buddha facing the wall

buddha facing the wall

Interviews with American Zen Monks

From the Zen Monastery Practice Center
under the guidance of Cheri Huber

Edited by Sara Jenkins

Publisher's Cataloging-in-Publication
(Provided by Quality Books, Inc.)

Buddha facing the wall : interviews with American Zen monks / from
    the Zen Monastery Practice Center under the guidance of
    Cheri Huber ; edited by Sara Jenkins. -- 1st ed.
        p. cm
        Preassigned LCCN: 98-67501
        ISBN: 0-9630784-3-7

    1. Buddhist monks--California--Interviews. 2. Zen
Buddhists--California--Interviews. 3. Monastic and
religious life (Zen Buddhism)--California. 4.
Spiritual life--Zen Buddhism. I. Jenkins, Sara. II.
Huber, Cheri. III. Zen Monastery Practice Center.

BQ9294.4.C3B83 1999   294.3'927'09794
                                 QBI98-1167

Permission has been requested from Penguin Putnam, Inc., to reprint the sentence quoted on p. 22 from Robert Thurman's *Inner Revolution: Life, Liberty, and the Pursuit of Real Happiness* (Riverhead Books, 1998).

The quotation from the Reverend Master Jiyu-Kennett on p. 19 is from a talk entitled "Perfect Faith" reprinted in *An Introduction to the Tradition of Serene Reflection Meditation* (Shasta Abbey Press, 1997).

Photography by William P. Gibson, Pocatello.

Design and cover by the Design Den, Denver/Pocatello.

Present Perfect Books
P. O. Box 1212, Lake Junaluska, NC 28745

W e say that the Monastery is a "privileged environment," meaning that everything about it is designed to support the spiritual practice of people who come here. A critical part of that is keeping our focus inward and allowing others to do the same, to avoid disturbing each other as we travel this path that leads to ending suffering.

The privileged environment is probably the most sacred aspect of the Monastery. It is the piece of the whole experience that people who train here are most devoted to, most appreciative of, most grateful for. We could go to other places and do retreats, but we wouldn't have the privileged environment. You have to come to a place like this to get a sense of how much more is possible when you are living in this way.

Cheri Huber

Contents

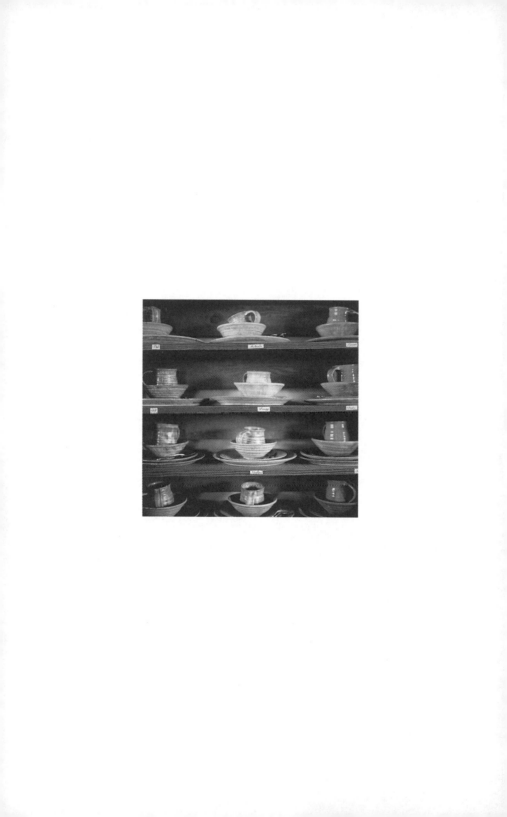

Preface

This book is based on interviews I conducted at the monastery under the guidance of Zen teacher Cheri Huber. Now called the Zen Monastery Practice Center (or simply "the Monastery"), it is located on three hundred acres in California's Sierra foothills, three hours east of San Francisco, in Calaveras County. It began as a rural retreat facility for the Zen Center Cheri founded in 1983 in Mountain View, California.

Cheri has taught meditation for over twenty years, beginning during her own monastic training in the Soto Zen tradition of Buddhism. Her many books and the retreats she leads at various centers draw students from around the country. Cheri's teaching style is renowned for its simplicity, openness, humor, and down-to-earth approach to transmuting life's difficulties into spiritual freedom.

My aim here is the same as in the three previous books that I edited and published on Cheri's teaching: as a long-time student of this gifted teacher, I wish to share some of the treasures I have discovered along this path. With this book on the Monastery, I also aim to present an unusual and particularly vibrant facet of a remarkable phenomenon, the flowering of Buddhist practice in Western culture. The perspective offered by monastic training seems to me particularly apt at this time, when Robert Thurman has so compellingly declared its importance not only in individual spiritual development but as a counterforce against the widespread violence and destruction that threaten life on earth (see his *Inner Revolution: Life, Liberty, and the Pursuit of Real Happiness*).

Interviews with the first of Cheri's students to live as Zen monks, along with a brief account of the first few years of the Monastery (1986-1990), appear in the initial book in this series, *Turning Toward Happiness: Conversations with a Zen Teacher and Her Students*. In subsequent interviews with monks over the last seven years, I distilled the questions I asked to these essentials: How did you come to spiritual practice, to this particular path, and to the Monastery, and what is it like? People who had responded to the first of those questions in previous interviews were asked simply, "What is it like now?" Recently, I also asked Cheri to talk about her own spiritual journey, putting the same questions to her.

The topics addressed in these personal accounts cover key elements in monastic practice, from silence and solitude, through various approaches to loosening the grip of ego, to some of the paradoxes characteristic of Zen teaching. These subjects are not presented in a systematic, expository manner, but simply as they occur in individuals' descriptions of monastic life and in interspersed excerpts from Cheri's talks.

Most of the people interviewed have spent several years at the Monastery. Others who lived there for extended periods are not represented here because they were not present on the three occasions (in 1992, 1996, and 1998) when the interviews were conducted. Transcripts of the interviews were sent to the monks for checking, correction, and approval. Of the seventeen people interviewed, all but one released their interviews for publication.

On reading their transcripts, some people were concerned about disparities between what they had said years earlier and their current understanding of Zen practice. Tricia said she came to terms with that by realizing that each interview is a snapshot of a particular moment in an ongoing, evolving spiritual journey. Still, my hope is that the interviews do convey something of the process involved: the repeated shifts, small and large, away from the unconscious bondage of egocentricity—clinging to the false idea that we are separate from everything else—and into the bright freedom of "letting go," being fully present, waking up.

Editing the interviews and making a book required much more letting go on my part than I had anticipated. The discovery that the amount of material I had gathered far exceeded what could feasibly be put into a book meant a painful decision: major text surgery. What is left, in most cases, are excerpts from much longer interviews. When forced to choose among parts that were equally appropriate within the framework of the book, I turned to a traditional method of ranking within Zen monasteries: seniority is determined neither by age nor spiritual attainment but by the date of entry into monkhood. Thus, in general, those who have been monks the longest are represented here by the longest interviews.

For me, the interviews evoke vivid images of sitting with and listening to each of the monks in the stillness of the Monastery: the individual traits expressed in voice and language and posture, the frequent laughter and occasional tears, the quality of the silences, the sincerity conveyed in the meeting of our eyes, the bond of sharing a 2,500-year-old meditation practice. Thus, the inevitable loss when speech is transposed into print seems especially acute here. My hope is that at least some of the transformative power of this practice comes through clearly in these glimpses into individual lives. As for the background material that I have written, it reflects my current understanding of this path, based on my own experience and what I have learned from the monks and from Cheri.

I am deeply grateful to the people I interviewed for talking so openly with me and for allowing me to use their words. I thank June Shiver for conducting the interview with Shonen. Surely I speak for the monks and countless others when I say that my deepest gratitude is to Cheri, who persistently turns our attention to the Buddha's Third Noble Truth, that ending suffering—and the natural happiness that results—is entirely possible, here and now.

In my experience, producing a book has always involved the same movement that is at the center of spiritual practice: from a fixed and restrictive preconception to something more open and more grounded, clearer and truer, in which the material itself determines the form. To allow that process to happen, I must relinquish my initial ideas about the book, even if that means starting over. At times I need serious nudges; fortunately, I can turn to my circle of compassionate critics. Leah Friedman, Kathryn Rogers, Jane Shuman, and Susan Stone helped me bring sharper focus and clearer structure to this material. Jeannie du Prau served as language consultant. Peter Phillips remains a steadfast source of support. Astute readers, brave commentators, and cherished companions on the spiritual path, each of these people played a valued role in encouraging me to do what needed to be done to move the material to a happier state than I had imagined possible.

May we all do whatever necessary to realize our True Nature and relish the happiness that brings! (Even if it means spending time in a monastery.)

Introduction: Facing the Wall

The monastic institution was, in a sense, invented by the Buddha. The first monastery comprised the men and women who gathered around him to learn the "middle way" between self-indulgence and self-denial, the path leading to liberation from the idea of the self as separate from all that is. The purpose of that first monastery was to offer a place in which individuals were free from the ordinary distractions of life to concentrate on developing their intelligence to the fullest, meaning to greater degrees of insight, wisdom, and compassion than would be possible otherwise.

The monastery described here continues that tradition. The guidelines and daily schedule in the last section of the book represent the foundation and framework that support the spiritual practice of people who come to train as monks.

As for the intervening millennia, plenty of books recount the history of Buddhism: its origins in North India; its spread, via the great monk Bodhidharma, to China in the late fifth to early sixth centuries and subsequently to Korea and Japan; its disappearance in the land of its birth and its centuries of flourishing in Southeast Asia and Tibet; the particular form developed in Japanese culture, Zen; and its coming to Europe and America in several waves during the last century, where it is evolving into new forms, mostly among lay practitioners. None of that, you may be relieved to know, will be

discussed here. Instead, this book presents a personalized view of a single, current manifestation of this phenomenon, the monastic training offered by Cheri Huber.

Questions of whether or not Buddhism is a religion and Zen a form of Buddhism have engaged such spiritual and intellectual giants as D. T. Suzuki and Thomas Merton; again, such issues are far beyond the scope of this book. My own exceedingly modest curiosity about these matters was troubled by one question, however, at the outset of my practice. Wanting to know what I was getting into (before realizing that that is the greatest, perhaps, of many unknowables), I asked Cheri if the meditation practice she teaches is necessarily "Buddhist." Her response, which was important in that it cleared my mind of that concern so that I could move on, was as follows:

> If you consider that the word "Buddha" simply means an "awakened" or "enlightened" being, then this practice is the process of waking up, and you can certainly use English words for that. I call it Buddhism myself (with some hesitation, because I wouldn't want anything I do to be held against Buddhism). I cannot communicate how much I treasure the teachings, how deeply I love and value this practice. Because it was made available for us by Gautama Buddha, I want to honor him. I'm also grateful to all of the people who continued this practice down through the years and kept it alive for us today, and using the term Buddhism is a way of acknowledging that.
>
> This is not to say that the Buddha was the only person ever to have attained the fully awakened state. But he went through a great deal of pain and suffering to have the experience that he had, and then he stayed with it long enough to develop it into a process that could be taught by one person to another person. That, to me, is remarkable.
>
> Nor is it to say that there aren't other paths people can

follow and also end suffering. But it is not my experience
that everything else works the same way. People love to say
about religion, "Well, it's all the same thing." When you
wake up, you realize that everybody who has awakened
does indeed experience the same thing, but the process of
getting to that point is not the same. What the Buddha
offered is a particular and highly effective system of ending
suffering.

And, you don't have to call it Buddhism. Certainly what
we are practicing has nothing to do with worship of the
Buddha.

Sometimes people say, isn't calling yourself a Buddhist
exclusionary? I don't see it that way. All I'm saying is that this
is the path that has given to me what I was looking for. This
is the process that has enabled me, to the degree that I
have, to go beyond suffering. Just for that, I will honor and
practice it for the rest of my life. And when I am no more,
I hope that whatever my practice has done to assist others
will go right on assisting them, in the way that not only
historical figures but regular folks walking around in life have
been a tremendous help to me in my practice. I hope I will
be thought of in exactly that way—just somebody who was
attempting to do a spiritual practice. What could be better
than that?

Making some of these same points is a small Buddha figure in
the meditation hall at the Monastery: like the meditators, it faces
the wall—a symbolic assertion that actual practice, not personhood,
is the focus of this tradition.

"Facing the wall" conveys to me the immediacy of "in your face"
and "up against the wall," expressions that might apply in difficult
stages of monastic training. At such times, there is nowhere to
turn; there is nothing to do but be fully present to your experience,
to face it. Facing our suffering is the first and unavoidable step in

the process of ending our suffering, which is what the Buddha discovered, taught, and offered to all beings. To me the significance of the phrase "facing the wall" is in the suggestion that there is nothing between oneself and the practice, no buffer, no protected zone in which to hide.

Within the inherent simplicity of Zen Buddhism, the practice at the Monastery is a particularly pared-down version. We have no special robes, no shaved heads, and next to no ritual (although we do bow a lot). Our foreign vocabulary consists of two Sanskrit words, *dharma* (teachings) and *sangha* (spiritual community), four or five Japanese words (for example, *sesshin,* an intensive meditation period), and a few Pali phrases, hesitantly intoned in the Daily Recollection that is recited each morning. While we meditate according to directions enunciated by the 13th-century master Dogen Zenji, and it is entirely possible that we sit in the very same way that Bodhidharma did (he is said to have spent nine years in meditation facing a wall), in Western Buddhism in general, Asian cultural forms tend to be dropped in favor of focusing on the essence of the practice. It is important to state that the heart of the path remains—in sharper relief, perhaps—as we attempt to follow the basic teachings of the Buddha, to look within ourselves to find the causes of suffering in the world.

We meditate with our eyes lowered but open. The blank expanse of wall in front of us is a reminder that the thoughts, emotions, memories, imaginary conversations, and the like that occupy us— here called "egocentricity," meaning the sense of being separate from everything else—are enacted entirely upon the inner screen of the mind. Produced by childhood training and social conditioning, as well as subtle and complex influences we cannot trace, these melodramas intrude on and interfere with our lives when we believe them to be true and unconsciously project them outward from ourselves. Our task in this spiritual practice is to observe these phantasms, the constructs of egocentricity, long enough to see through their insubstantial nature. Once we cease to identify with our mental activity, cease to allow it to define who we are, we begin to live from something that is true and deep and connected to all. Once we have faced the fierce attachments of egocentricity and dispelled their power, there is nothing left but what is right here, right now: the wall in front of our eyes, the sensation of sitting on the cushion, the sounds around us, our breathing—and all of existence. Then, "facing the wall" simply signifies the practice of sitting meditation.

At the Monastery, another form of blank expanse is the silence. In this, it is atypical; most monasteries observe silence only during certain periods. Here, communication is restricted to the essential and is directed to the spiritual guide or the monk in charge of the relevant aspect of operation (generally the work director or guestmaster) through notes on a central bulletin board. The exceptions are a weekly group discussion among the monks, discussions within the context of retreats or special workshops, "functional" talking when necessary in work situations, and, of course, meeting with the teacher.

All of this serves the process of freeing oneself from ego-centricity, or the "conditioned mind," as it is also called (for short, "conditioning" or even "ego," though the latter term is used differently in psychology). Monastic renunciation may seem to involve primarily material and social pleasures and the distractions of the normal world, but what is ultimately renounced—and this is the whole point—is egocentricity. Monks relinquish a great deal of personal choice: they carry out whatever tasks they are assigned, they eat what is served, they refrain from complaint and even opinion. Within this framework, it becomes easier to discern the workings of ego: the urges to assert and defend the self, to gain some (illusion of) control. The next step is to free oneself from those conditioned patterns of thought and behavior, to gradually discover a way of living more fully in the richness of each moment. The monastery provides a setting in which to gradually turn over the directing of one's life to something other than the illusion of a separate self. In Cheri's words,

> The teacher's role is to take egocentricity away from you. Where you might give in to egocentricity, I won't let that happen, which allows you to have an experience of going beyond it.
>
> Here's an example of how that works most often in our monastery, and in the monastery where I trained (those are the only two monastic experiences I know). If you come to the Monastery to train, I would already know you pretty well; I would know what you liked and what you didn't like, and I would know what you're afraid of. So, what we would start working on, slowly, is putting you in situations where you are required to face your fear. A monastery is a safe place in which to discover how to go beyond egocentricity and to experience freedom you cannot know until you do.

The relationship between spiritual teacher and student is unique in human society and is often misunderstood. In addressing this topic, the late Zen Master Jiyu-Kennett, founder of the Order of Buddhist Contemplatives and first Abbess of Shasta Abbey (and a teacher whose influence Cheri often acknowledges), distinguished between "perfect faith" and "absolute faith."

> Far too many people feel that, if you come to a monastery, you have to give up your will and blindly follow everything you are told. Perfect faith, however, does not require this. What it *does* require is that you accept everything with a positive attitude of mind. Absolute faith, which is a requirement of many religions, differs from perfect faith in that "absolute" implies a hardness, with no means whatsoever of allowing for softness or change. . . .

She goes on to say that if the teacher requires a student to surrender his or her own will, then the relationship is not a spiritual one. If, on the other hand, the teacher asks the student to have perfect faith in something that is greater than both teacher and student, which is the "true master," that something should not be construed as a god or other entity. Rather, in Jiyu-Kennett's words, "it is the essence of all things; totally empty, the fullest emptiness."

In a discussion at a meditation retreat (in 1992), Cheri gave a concrete example of the positive attitude of mind, or "perfect faith," that is required of a monk.

> I just talked with the monks today, and the question arose, who will go to the San Francisco airport to meet someone who is flying in for a stay at the Monastery? Phyl is scheduled to go down to Mountain View to lead guidance, and Greg is busy with the building, and Jennifer can't go because she's driving the tractor.
>
> I loved hearing that. Jennifer was a Montessori school teacher before she became a monk, and I can tell you that the last thing in the world she thought she would be doing when she came to the Monastery was driving a tractor. Another woman there had never cooked before in her life—she thought cooking was canned soup and peanut butter sandwiches—and it just worked out that we didn't have a cook for a thirty-day retreat, and a week before, she became the cook. She learned on the job by cooking for twenty-five people. Once she got through that, if someone had said, "You want to be an astronaut?" she'd have said, "Sure, nothing to it." Greg is in charge of construction for the building. When he came four years ago, I don't think he'd ever nailed two boards together.
>
> So, today on the phone, trying to rearrange things so someone could drive to the airport, I said to Cameron, "Why don't you go down to Mountain View and lead guidance?" She said, "I'm not good at that. I tried it once

before, and I don't think I can do it." I said, "Great. This will be a wonderful chance for you to develop those skills. Get in the car."

My ongoing encouragement to people is to do more and more outrageous things, and those who have been willing to go along on this ride will tell you that it can get pretty outrageous. Four people are up there in the mountains building this huge building all by themselves, and they are so involved in it that they don't even know another life is possible. When Sara interviewed them about it, she kept asking questions about when the building would be finished, and they just kept talking about the *process* of building. That's their entire focus, and that's their spiritual practice: they get up in the morning and go to the work site and build the building and do their best to stay present to all of their experience.

The point is that it's only through that kind of steadfast pursuit that we're willing or able to break through our limitations. We look out from the barriers we have erected around ourselves—the prison of egocentricity—and wonder, why doesn't my life work? But that gets us nowhere. We have to see the barriers clearly and then push against them. There's no way we can push and maintain those barriers at the same time. It's one of those wonderful laws of nature: if you continue to push, eventually you'll push through to freedom.

Because the teacher-student relationship is critically important to this path, Cheri accepts no more than ten monks at a time. Thus, while the Monastery has expanded rapidly in the twelve years of its existence, especially in terms of accommodations for retreatants, the number of monks never exceeds ten.

In response to questions about life at the Monastery, the following was published in the Zen Center/Monastery newsletter under the heading "Who Are the Monks?"

Monks are men and women who have seen that it is possible to awaken and end suffering in this lifetime and are committed to doing that.

A monk has glimpsed her own "treasure house," has seen "the pearl of great price," and is willing to do whatever is necessary to be at one with that. A monk is willing to let go. No matter how many times he loses his focus, gets identified, falls into conditioning, he grasps his willingness to drop it all and come back to the breath. He doesn't waste his precious opportunity by indulging in self-recriminations for being a conditioned human.

Monks pay attention. They pay attention while they eat, meditate, work, sleep. They keep silent. They acknowledge, accept, and embrace what is. They breathe in and out. They embrace willingness with every breath.

We have many guidelines at the Monastery, but only one rule: we will use everything in our experience to see how we cause ourselves to suffer and to let go of that in order to end suffering. A monk's commitment is to follow this rule moment by moment.

◇

Negative preconceptions of monks and monasteries are common in our culture. Yet it is also common that in the company of long-term Buddhist monks, people sense extraordinary degrees of calm, gentleness, generosity, lightheartedness, and ease, which melt away the stereotypes of losers and misfits, deprivation and denial. It is no great thing, perhaps, that the archetypal Buddhist monk embodies those most appealing of human attributes; more significant is how actual monks can seem so fully themselves, so deeply at one with exactly who they are. "Never has there been," Robert Thurman says in *Inner Revolution,* "before or since the Buddha's teachings, a more positive philosophy nor one that cherishes the individual quite so much."

Misery is easier to describe, of course, than joy, and the monks interviewed for this book did not shrink from the task of recounting their suffering from heat, cold, work, and ongoing challenges to egocentricity, including the obligation to share space with other creatures. For example, the Monastery is located in the path of an annual tarantula migration, and the unwelcome proximity of spiders loomed large in some accounts of the hardships of monastic life. Facing obstacles is fundamental to the process the monks are practicing, however, and so they relate their difficulties with the good humor that comes from a larger spiritual perspective.

The symbolic significance of spiders was, regrettably, too fragile to survive the journey from spoken word to printed page, so I'll just have to tell it straight out: to me, spiders are perfect representations of the creepier dark corners of the psyche that are revealed in silence and solitude. Meditation can be likened to penetrating those corners with the light of awareness and learning to accept, with equanimity and compassion, whatever is found there. It is precisely that acceptance that frees us from living lives constricted by fear of what might be discovered in us and opens us to the joy of loving everything that we are.

◇

In Buddhism, people may enter a monastery for varying lengths of time, and it is common to undertake regular periods of monastic training. Under certain conditions, a person may reside at a monastery without becoming a monk, and accommodations often are available for guests. At the monastery described in this book, celibacy is not a rule, but sexual relations are precluded by the guidelines on silence, solitary living, and no personal interaction (which includes keeping "custody of the eyes," meaning no eye contact and not looking at others), except when it is required by work or in discussion groups.

Although this monastery offers one particular style of practice among many, it seems to me to embody the essential elements of traditional Zen monastic life: a rigorous schedule of sitting and walking meditation and work (considered a third form of meditation), with personal spiritual guidance from the teacher. At this monastery, however, becoming a monk does not involve accepting a more extensive set of precepts than those given to lay practitioners. The ten basic precepts (which vary in wording, but in this tradition are roughly equivalent in content to the Ten Commandments) are taken as vows each morning. They are treated not as rules but as guidelines that support the effort toward awakening, and they may change and deepen in their implications as one's spiritual practice evolves.

The following description from the Monastery guidebook gives a sense of the aim and some of the fundamental means of monastic training.

This privileged environment is a place where those seeking oneness with all that is can gather and practice together. It is a place where everything is designed, with the greatest compassion, to provide the opportunity to awaken and live from our True Nature. Here our hearts can learn to open without fear of intrusion or interference from without, where each person is encouraged to risk being her or his most vulnerable self.

The privileged environment facilitates the inward focus of spiritual practice by encouraging us to look at the processes of life and to expose to the light of awareness and attention the belief systems of social conditioning and the suffering they cause.

The "still, small voice within" has been drowned out by our conditioning, by books, TV, movies, relationship struggles, social pressures—all of the distractions that feed ego while starving our True Nature. The silence of the Monastery gives that voice the opportunity to be heard.

Silence of mouth, of eye, of movement, and of mind are all encouraged by the practice, by the guidelines, and by the physical setting of the Monastery. Silence has the effect of helping us look inward and be in our surroundings in a way which avoids disturbing others and their inward journeys.

Necessary communication is written or whispered. Eye contact is discouraged, as is watching others as they go about their day. No feeling of being watched, no sense of another's questioning eyes asking, "Who are you?" Less opportunity to search with our eyes for approval, for recognition, for reflection of false self.

We are asked to be mindful as we open and close doors, as we eat, as we move about the building and property, and we are given guidelines which support mindfulness.

"Return to the breath," we are encouraged over and over and over again, and it is the breath of compassion which most inspires our privileged environment. From it flows the understanding that we are each adequate to our own experience—no need to be "helped" as we grope along our way; that the tasks we are assigned are for our spiritual training and doing them quickly or "right" or even getting them done is not the point; that we are each capable of going beyond who we believe we are—and we will be asked to do so; that self-hate is not helpful; that there truly is nothing wrong with anyone, with anything.

What is asked of those who have gathered in the privileged environment is the willingness to use everything in our experience to see how we cause ourselves to suffer so that we may drop that and end suffering. We are asked to show up, to pay attention, to be willing to say "yes" to each opportunity as it is offered.

Just as compassion is the breath of the privileged

environment, the *sangha*—that collection of seekers who share this path—is its body; it is the *sangha,* each of its members, that gives the practice its form, its viability. "In this way I do most deeply vow to train myself" is spoken by each member, shared by all.

◇

Conducting these interviews has offered me many opportunities to observe my own egocentricity in action and, on occasion, to go beyond it.

The original interviews (published in *Turning Toward Happiness*) took place in a somewhat spontaneous manner on my first visit to the Monastery. The next visit, however, was preceded by weeks of mounting anxiety. My impression was that the monks were busy every minute of the day and any departure from their schedule would not happen casually. Yet I was unable to find out from Cheri exactly when I would be able to speak with them. It occurred to me that she was deliberately testing my equanimity, but I could not refrain from pressing for information.

"You mean I'm coming two thousand miles to do these interviews, and I can't schedule a specific time to do them?" I asked, incredulous.

Such wheedling left Cheri unfazed. "When you arrive," she told me firmly, "you can work out a time with Greg. He is the work director, and he schedules the monks' activities."

In retrospect, waiting until I arrived to make a plan sounds entirely reasonable, but anxiety is notoriously unimpressed by reason. The point is that instead of trying to persuade or placate me, Cheri allowed me to *have* the full experience of unreasonable fear. Now, that type of gift often goes unappreciated the first time it is offered, and it took me a while to understand its import.

As soon as I got to California, I called Greg and explained my urgent need to know what was going to happen and when. Greg laughed and said something like, "I have a sense of what you're going through. Being in charge of this construction project, I get anxious about other people not meeting my timetable. But I can only pass along a thought that I use as a reminder for myself to keep things in perspective: 'There are many hours in the day, and I am not indispensable'."

I earnestly scribbled down those words (and still have the note on my desk) but despaired of ever internalizing their wisdom.

So, I went to the Monastery with no idea how the interviewing would be done and fearing the worst, namely, that it would not happen at all. When I got there, however, the monks stopped their work, and we did a group interview. It was so simple, so easy. I remember experiencing a softening, physical as well as mental, once I abandoned the idea that I had to take charge and make it all happen.

A year later, spending several nights at the Monastery on my way home from a retreat, it seemed natural to conduct individual interviews with the four people living there as monks at that time. It happened without any problem. I remembered: I could turn it into a source of anxiety, or not—my choice.

In 1996, the number of monks had grown to ten, and when I came for a longer period to conduct interviews, I was confident, relaxed—complacent, really, which is always dangerous in Zen practice. At a preliminary meeting, I said I hoped we would resist the temptation to slip into interviewer/interviewee roles; I would try to drop expectations about what a monk would say and hoped they would drop any effort to fulfill such expectations.

One of the monks suggested that the interviews be conducted with the same attentiveness that is brought to guidance sessions with the teacher, and that we follow formal procedure: each monk would come at an appointed time (for an hour each), and we would sit on meditation cushions facing each other. I agreed, although I had envisioned us lolling about comfortably in the newly opened dormitory, chatting seriously but informally. Formality seemed to imply some solemn, unspoken requirements that I feared I could not meet. Yet, as so often happens, the difficulty I encountered led me into entirely new territory.

One person (whose interview was not released) began by stating that he had not wanted to participate. He had come only because he had been urged to as part of his spiritual practice, in order to recognize that the interview was simply another experience that he could pay attention to and possibly learn from. Before we started, he requested that we speak "monk to monk," meaning that I too would commit myself to being as present, as attentive as possible, every moment.

Because I am not a monk, and because I held the idea that monkhood automatically confers spiritual superiority, I was uncertain and apprehensive. Things got worse when he expressed skepticism about the usefulness of books in general and interviews in particular. Indeed, he was skeptical about the whole notion of anybody helping anybody else. I was thoroughly intimidated. I saw no alternative, however, to sitting on my cushion, facing him, listening to what he said, and being honest in my responses.

We spent long stretches of that hour in silence. Again and again, with every breath, it seemed, I consciously chose to be present, not to slip off into fear of what might happen or fantasies of escape, but to be at ease in that situation. My constant support was the lesson in Cheri's having allowed me to experience the full intensity of my anxiety in the past: I knew for myself, in my own body, that such tension was unnecessary, an easily avoidable form of suffering, and that I could simply let it go. When the present fear returned, which it did, with almost every breath, I saw it too as a support. The fear demanded that I be totally alert, and I listened more intently than I had ever listened to anything. As a result, I heard in what the man said something that he appeared to have difficulty in hearing for himself.

After one particularly long silence, punctuated by a few halting remarks from him, he asked if I could help him understand what was going on, "monk to monk." I have an aversion to the counselor/ therapist/spiritual guide role that involves listening and reflecting back to another person. Normally, I would have said that I could not help, or I would have offered glib advice before finding a way to escape. But monks are expected to "be willing to say 'yes' to each opportunity as it is offered." So, I did my best to remain fully present and to respond to whatever arose, to stay soft.

I heard myself telling him simply what I took to be the essence of his own words, and I could see in his face that something struck home. My words seemed to illuminate his experience so that he could see it more clearly. In that moment, I felt, we were experiencing the same thing, and the words that hung in the air between us appeared as simple truth, to which neither of us had exclusive claim and to which both of us contributed.

At the end of the interview, I realized that, while I had "helped" him, he too had helped me. By requiring my attention, and, by directly asking me to respond, he had challenged me to do and be something utterly beyond what I thought myself capable of. I turned off the tape recorder and told him that, remarking that our experience together seemed to answer the question about people's ability to be helpful to one another: each of us, despite our expectations, had helped the other. We looked at each other in silence, our eyes filled with tears.

With each interview, in fact, I began to see more clearly into the person facing me. I could see the human goodness and sincerity and effort, see it shining right through their struggles, their fits of hating the place and the other monks and the teacher and wondering why they were there. And I could see too that those qualities and contradictions and potential exist within me as well, that "being a monk" is available to anyone, that they and I are, at heart, the same.

Openness

Outside the window of my dormitory room, two deer rest in the spacious shelter of a live oak. Their tranquil symmetry reminds me of the deer in ancient Buddhist art: the Buddha's first sermon, it is said, was preached in a deer park.

Behind the deer, the long branches of the tree bow to the ground, sweep outward, and rest there, as if to offer a protected place for these gentle creatures, without confining them. That is what the Monastery is for us.

Everywhere I notice the same graceful movement. The lines of the main monastery building spread from the tiled roofs down through redwood piers then outward along broad porches and open walkways stretched across the ground. And yet again: from this high point on the land, paths radiate down through rolling hills and meadows, branching off to fifteen private hermitages, each hidden among pine, oak, toyon, and manzanita.

Like the spiritual practice it serves—which takes us down into the depth of our being, then releases us out to the world—the Monastery is a refuge that stands wide open.

"Openness" may not immediately come to mind as a quality associated with monasticism. And yet, the opening of mind and heart is central to the spiritual training offered here. These Zen monks do not take lifetime vows; instead, they accept the challenge of bringing full awareness to the ever-changing present. Their aim is to wake up from the delusion and dissatisfaction of ego-driven lives, their practice is to look deeply into experience, and their commitment is to remain open to whatever is encountered. In every aspect of its functioning, the Monastery is designed to support continual opening within each person. Thus, openness is at once goal, process, and attainment.

Part of Buddhism's appeal in the West is its openness to other religions. Among the seventeen people interviewed for this book, four are practicing Roman Catholics. One of them, Lois, left a job she had held for eighteen years to spend a year at the Monastery as a way of deepening her Christianity. In place of an image of God, she felt, Buddhism (though generally considered nontheistic) offers an *experience* of God, and Lois wanted that know experience for herself. Cheri's attitude that having the experience is what is important, not what we call it, opened the door for Lois to spend a year as a Zen monk.

During her first few weeks at the Monastery, Lois felt some concern that in making such a major commitment to Zen practice, her religious faith might be weakened. On the other hand, she reasoned, if her faith was truly precious to her, it would not be lost. "After all," she said, "my faith is what got me here. I didn't come because of Buddhism."

Many of us do come, though, because of that characteristic openness, not only to religious faiths but in a much deeper and broader sense. The openness of this path not only gives us room to be who we already think we are, it allows us to realize that we are more, far beyond our ideas of what is possible.

◇

Phyllis

Phyl began studying with Cheri in 1982 and was one of the first three people to live at the Monastery. A Sister of Notre Dame, Phyl had lived for twenty-three years in spiritual community when she received permission from her order to pursue full-time training as a Zen monk. This interview began with my request that Phyl repeat something she had said about enlightenment at a recent Zen-Catholic retreat.

1992

Enlightenment? We are all enlightened. We abide in enlightenment. Our task is to realize that. Perhaps it is being aware of the humanness and the divinity of us at the same time, aware of our conditioning and our true nature all at once. Aware and willing to experience what is there in any given moment. Perhaps it is the same as union.

I always wondered what union meant—union of what? I finally figured out that it means union of wills. It's when the struggling stops, when the resistance stops. Struggle and separation are the same thing. In Christian terms, there is God's will, "Thy will be done." In Buddhist terms, it's letting our will go along with the universe, being open and available and ready for what's next. To me, that is what enlightenment must be. There are different words for the same experience: oneness, or clarity, because you're not muddled by the struggle, the separateness, the suffering. I know that experience in myself: as soon as I come back to the breath and stop resisting life, there is clarity.

Christian scriptures describe losing your life to gain it. Some teachers understand that to mean dying physically and going to heaven. Others understand it to mean the process that we talk about in Buddhism. That is, there are certain stages in this path when you think you're dying, literally, but it's the ego gasping its last breath. In Christian terms, death leads to resurrection, and we can also call this experience "transformation." Dying and being reborn, so to speak, is something we experience in our lives whenever we let go. To me, that's what resurrection is about. Because humans have that experience of letting go, dying and arising again, this concept is found in all religions.

I like the term "awakening"; that's easier for me to grasp than enlightenment. Awakening is a process that starts and grows, and you just get clearer and clearer. It also can happen in each moment, as we drop each moment and move onto the next, finish each breath and move onto the next. As we become more aware, we begin to see that we're actually a different person in each moment. It's just ordinary life; but then ordinary life, walking around living and breathing, takes on a different meaning. And to me that's exciting— it's the most exciting thing that ever existed.

1996

The last two years have been a time of huge change for me. Cheri has been so supportive in a very—ah, strong way, shall we say. Several years ago, at a low point, I said to her, "Do whatever you can to get me over the hump, to get me to the other side."

Hard training went on for about two years. One example of how it worked was in a crisis situation. Something very difficult happened, something very painful, which directly affected me, and I really wanted to discuss it with Cheri and the other people involved. But you can't talk to anybody else here, and Cheri was away, and she didn't come, she didn't come, she didn't come, for three weeks. For a while, not discussing what felt like a crisis became even more difficult than the original issue, and getting through that was major work. Then, when Cheri was about to return, we set up a meeting of the people involved, and I don't know whether she forgot or decided it wasn't necessary for me to be present or what, but the meeting was scheduled for a time when I wouldn't be there—they were going to have the meeting without me, and I was a key player! In the end, I was at the meeting. I was very grateful for that whole experience: not being able to talk with anybody, not being able to reach Cheri, not being included in plans—all that was essential to the process I went through within myself. Eventually, I did reach acceptance, at a deeper level than I had experienced before.

For several weeks after that incident, I felt very different. Even though things were still difficult and painful, I was able to trust that that was exactly what needed to be. And it was, because a change took place in me. I don't know how to describe it except to say that whatever it is that happens in spiritual training happened then; whatever happens when you stay with your own pain, sit with it, fully allow it to be whatever it is, then release it, no right/wrong, no good/bad—that happened. You come out on the other side, and it's like emerging from a cocoon and becoming a butterfly.

It's not that Cheri thought, "For me not to be at the Monastery right now will be perfect for Phyl's training." She was just off leading retreats and workshops in other places. Now that I'm in charge of the day-to-day training for the other people here, it's clear to me how it works: whatever happens—mistakes and oversights and whatever I do just living life—are perfect opportunities for the others to deal with in their practice.

I have faith and trust in the guide [Cheri in her role as teacher; also can refer to anyone who takes on the teaching role, which monks may as part of their training] as an instrument of the universe. The trust in the teacher is not trust that she knows something I don't, it's trust that the universe manifests through her. Whether it appears to be neglect on her part or guidance that is right on target, it's always been absolutely perfect. It's not that I think she doesn't make mistakes, it's that I trust that the good of the universe will come through even in what seem to be mistakes. The teacher's job is to be attuned to the universe, to love unconditionally, to have no vested interest in what's going on, and the student's job is to trust. Having complete trust has been to my advantage, in the sense that there's nothing else to hold on to. No matter how hard things got for me, I trusted.

I think it would work even if the teacher were a little shaky and the student still trusted completely, because it's the *trust* that never lets you down. The trust isn't in Cheri as a person, the trust is in myself, and that trust goes through Cheri, as the guide, to the universe. There's trust that no matter what happens, I have the wherewithal to use all of my experience as an opportunity to awaken.

I'm pretty convinced that to do spiritual training, that trust has to be there. How could you train with a teacher and then question her? The feeling of "I'm right, they're wrong" is ego stuff; to allow even the smallest bit of that is letting ego be in control. I'm not talking about being blindly obedient, but trusting that whatever happens is for my training—and within that trust, it is. Not only that, but within the trust a lot of the transformation happens, because to have that much faith and trust *is* the transformation.

About two years ago, at another low point, I was driving back from taking someone to the train station, and I felt some movement, like a bubble inside me. There was a sense of, "I can do it! I can do it!" Meaning, "I can do whatever is required of me in the moment. I can say 'yes' to life." (This is all grace, of course.) Now, only the day before, I couldn't do it. I wasn't enough for myself; I still needed outside intervention, I needed to be "saved" by someone or something beyond myself. But that day I knew: I *could* do it. When I got back, I went to Cheri and said, *"I can do it!"* Then she was like a wholly different person, because she was talking to a whole different person. She was no longer talking to an ego-controlled, depressed, miserable person who thinks they can't do it. She was talking to a person who—*can* do it!

From then on, nothing was hard, the resistance just wasn't there.

As long as it's hard, you can know that's ego resisting. As soon as you're present to whatever is, even though it may not be pleasant or the way you want it, there's no longer that hardness of resistance, that suffering.

I would have been content to spend the rest of my life as a quiet monk, just doing what I was told to do. But Greg and Jennifer had left, which meant there were only two of us here, then Cameron was diagnosed with cancer, and right after that my mother had cancer, so I had to accept many more responsibilities—more than I would have dreamed this person could handle. I've taken on the jobs of guestmaster and work director when Mary's not here and spiritual guide when Cheri's not here. And it's fine, because there is no resistance. I think resistance is a cover-up for fear: fear that someone will judge me, fear that I'll be too uncomfortable, fear that I'll fail. I always had been afraid to take responsibility. But at some point, instead of turning away from myself to try to figure out what somebody else expected, I looked within myself to see what needed to be done—which is much easier. Once that is established, everything is a piece of cake.

The first six or seven years here were extremely difficult, but when you walk through the "gateless gate"—and that's exactly what it's like when you stop resisting: there's this gate, and you can't get through it, you can't get through it, you can't get through it, and then all of a sudden, you look back and there's no gate—then it's bliss. Oh, it still gets hot, there are too many bugs, work is hard, I still get depressed and want not to be depressed. Yet I can stay with myself, stay with the sensations in my body, and that makes all the difference.

Practice definitely continues on both sides of the gate. In fact, it never ends. You always have to watch, ever more closely, because if you give ego an inch, it takes a mile. I think of ego, or conditioning, as being like gravity: it exerts this constant pull on you, and mostly we live our lives completely unaware of it.

Here it's so much easier because of the quiet, the space, just being left alone in the midst of some difficulty, so that when the conditioning appears, we are better able to see it. It's not something we can learn once and be done with it. It takes time and focus to look, look, look at what ego is and how it works. Here we have a chance to experiment with our conditioning, our identities, to really get to know ego. Here we don't have the constant support for ego that you do in the outside world; we have only the internal support in our own heads. The Monastery is set up so it's easier to do this hard thing, this very subtle thing, of learning to discern what is conditioning and what is not.

Even a person who doesn't come to a monastery can take their spiritual practice with them, like a turtle with its own monastery on its back, so to speak. We can always go to a place within ourselves that is like a monastery: silent and peaceful and devoted to practice, where our relationship with ourselves involves respectful and compassionate questioning. It takes practice, but just knowing that it exists inside, that we don't have to look it for externally, is reassuring. The whole realization in Zen is that there is no separation: we already are what we're looking for. We are all of it, we just haven't noticed.

The more my eyes are opened, the more I see that really I don't know anything. And yet, the ability grows to just do what has to be done, without wavering. I don't see anything ahead, so in that sense I don't know what my path is, but as soon as I put my foot down, it's there. It's like magic: I don't see anything except this moment, but I keep taking the next step, and, sure enough, the path is there.

The "gateless gate" refers to a paradigm shift, from everything being wrong to nothing being wrong. Passing through the gate is finding out that the paradigm we live in is a illusion: it's not true that there's something wrong. The shift to seeing things as they are is like taking off a pair of glasses: wearing the "something wrong" glasses, life is hard, but once we take them off—ah, so *this* is how life is!

Especially, you see that there's nothing wrong with yourself, because there's no self-hate to be projected inward or outward. You're your own best friend, you become your own constant companion. Christians call this the presence of God. Within that, life goes on—ups and downs, heat and bugs, depression and pain—but there's not that separation.

My companion has taken off now and then for a minute or an hour or even a day, but I know what's going on, and when that companion comes back, I am so grateful to feel the connection restored. It feels like a real person here with me, but it is just me coming back to me. Then I can be grateful for the experience of the separation itself, because having gotten used to the companionship, I forget what it was like without it.

I didn't ask God to make me a Zen Buddhist. I didn't plan my life to work out this way. I could never have dreamed up this good a life for myself. So I'll sing the praises of this practice until my dying day. Because it works—and anybody who knows from whence I came, they can *see* that it works. As e. e. cummings said, "I thank You God . . . for everything, which is natural which is infinite which is yes (i who have died am alive again today and this is the sun's birthday, and this is the birth day of life and of love and of wings . . .)." That's how life seems. It's still life doing life, but it's really wonderful being in the garden doing life rather than being outside banging on the gate and waiting for life to start.

2

Intimate and Nonpersonal

Within the silence, within the keeping-to-oneself of monastic life, a powerful sense of community can arise. Unlike ordinary community, it is not based on interests, abilities, personality, or social status. At the Monastery, monks may work, eat, and meditate together for years without knowing one another's last names or personal history. Their bonds include those of proximity and shared struggle, certainly, but more important is an indescribable bond of spirit that links those who follow the same path toward liberation.

In 1991, five years after the first monks began living there full time, the Monastery was still referred to as "the land." That term suggests to me the crucial shift that happens in spiritual practice, from assuming ourselves to be central and separate to sensing our coexistence within a larger, nonpersonal context. At the Monastery that shift can happen more readily than elsewhere. We turn from seeing ourselves as major performers and everything else as accompaniment (with occasional rude eruptions from weather, wildlife, and other "acts of God") to allowing our species and its affairs to settle into supporting roles. We are called upon occasionally to sing our individual songs, as it were, but mostly we hum along in harmony with the ongoing symphony of all that is.

Such a deeply integrated way of being was evoked for me whenever the monks spoke of "the land." The land is what was here before we came and will remain when we are gone, the ever-evolving matrix from which arise the possibilities for human development in a given place.

At the time of those first interviews, group activities—meals and meditation—still took place in two large Army surplus tents, with outhouses and outdoor showers for private functions; light came from kerosene lamps and flashlights, and water was bottled. On a hilltop meadow near the entrance, however, foundations had been laid for a building to house kitchen, dining hall, and dormitory, and the rammed-earth walls were under construction. The four people who were monks at that time met with me for a group interview at the work site, where "functional" talking was allowed.

Even with the disturbances of earth-moving, jack-hammering, and concrete-pouring, the monks seemed very aware of their interconnectedness with the land. One sign of that was an increased sensitivity to sharing the habitats of other creatures. One monk told how the tractor is stopped to allow a tarantula to make its way to safety, another how someone carrying boards carefully steps over a trail of ants each time she goes back and forth between the lumber yard and the building site.

In mid-August 1992, that awareness of interconnection was acutely intensified when forest fire approached the Monastery. On the second day of the annual Zen-Catholic retreat Cheri was leading at Carmel, news came that eighty percent of the fire was uncontrolled, and 55,000 acres were already lost. A few days later, the fire had reached the edge of the Monastery property, and the monks and animals were evacuated. Cheri and Phyl, who were co-leading the retreat, seemed calm as they relayed news from the daily phone reports, although Phyl did admit to a sleepless night.

On the final day of the retreat, we learned that the fire had been controlled and the monks had returned. Two of us stayed at the Monastery on our way home. By the time we arrived, the weather had cooled, and the only trace of fire was the lingering smell of smoke and a blackened hillside across the canyon. But one variety of pine trees seemed to be dying, and the stark limbless trunks were a haunting reminder that against the forces of disease and destruction, many of the life forms on the land are fragile indeed, and all the more precious.

Greg, one of the first of Cheri's students to become a monk, had been living at the Monastery for five years when the forest fire approached. He described that experience.

All of us who practice here as monks realized that in a way we already knew we could lose the place any time, for so many reasons: we can't pay for it, everybody leaves, or a fire. Then the fire actually started coming.

For me, it was another opportunity to keep doing the practice. The fire is coming, so we ask ourselves, what needs to be done? We said, let's get some clothes for everybody and get some tools we don't want to lose and pack up the cars. We didn't know if we were going to have to leave or not, and days went by that way, with all of us just doing whatever needed to be done. Jennifer fixed lunch. Mark started a painting project, knowing that it might never get finished.

That experience made it very clear that what we do in this moment has nothing to do with what's going to happen in the next moment, and that it's possible to live that way. We could have identified with people who were worried and hysterical and afraid of losing stuff, but we just did what we'd been practicing for a long time. What's on the schedule? What's next? When it's time to meditate, go meditate. If it's time to prepare for evacuation, do that.

There wasn't any sense of it being a breach of faith to pack up some clothes because that would mean we were attached to belongings. Why not do the sensible thing and pack up some clothes? On the other hand, it wasn't as if we

were irresponsible because we weren't frantically trying to carve a 300-foot firebreak around the building. Cheri's perspective on it was really clear: she said she'd rather have the building burn and the trees spared than the trees burn and the building spared, because we could always rebuild the building.

Doing what's intelligent isn't the same as operating out of fear. When I was first assigned to be in charge of the building project, I would get very upset about things that might happen about permits and regulations and building officials. It took a long time to realize that I didn't have the slightest idea what was going to happen, and that to make preparations against what I was afraid was going to happen was crazy.

When the fire came close, we did have to leave for several days. When we came back, we continued with our practice in the same way. The next thing was to clean up, to get the ashes out of the buildings so we could move back in.

$$\diamondsuit$$

A seeming contradiction in these interviews is that the monks' accounts of their experience can sound somewhat impersonal, despite the fact that, as several of them mention, living together in silence feels "intimate." To me, this suggests how, paradoxically, the monastic way of life fulfills the Buddhist vow to work for the salvation of all beings: the impersonality reflects a waning of the illusion of the self as separate from all that is, and the concomitant development of a willingness to act in the interest of all. Through the intensified awareness and the deeper participation in life that result from monastic training, connections among beings can be experienced as a growing sense of intimacy. This was addressed in a group discussion following one session of interviews.

Mary: In the interview, I realized that talking about my life here was hard for me. It's very intimate, just to live here. We could talk about the same things somewhere else, but the intimacy is much broader here. I don't know how to express that any other way.

Sara: I also became aware of that quality of intimacy. During the interviews, I was having the experience of us both hearing the same thing, regardless of which person was speaking. Sitting on the cushions and facing each other, and the presence of the other person—something about that called on me also to be doing my practice in each moment. Even though one person was talking more, the process was happening between us, it wasn't a one-way thing. So, if I'm going to thank you for something, it's not only for your being intimate, but also for allowing me to be.

Cheri: That's what I love about this practice. When I sit with people, doing guidance, I'm not sitting there guiding them, I'm sitting there being guided by the experience. I have to really *be* there, fully engaged, every second. And that kind of presence is powerful.

Phyllis: What I notice is that intimacy is part and parcel of *what is*. It's part of the intrinsic being of the universe. Life *is* intimate unless we're separating ourselves from it; intimacy is another word for unity or oneness. If we think of ourselves as separate beings, we attach a different connotation to it, choosing to be "intimate" with one special person or a few. But that's just trying to fill up a hole that wouldn't even be there if we weren't holding ourselves separate from everything.

Cheri: When we are caught in the illusion of separateness, we have to "make" friends. Otherwise, we would just *be* friends.

Phyllis: So, Zen involves dropping the idea of separateness, that illusion, and realizing that all is intimate, all is friendship.

Cheri: Yes; realizing, "I live here, I belong here, I'm part of all this." What we cling to as a reason for our separateness is the belief that there's something wrong with us. We have to keep up the walls that define us as separate, because otherwise people will see our flaws and find out who we really are.

In the monastic environment, to the degree that we don't know one another as personalities, we have no information about each other to attach to the beliefs and opinions and attitudes that support that separation. All we see is that this person has given up what they were doing to come here and do spiritual practice, in this very difficult way of life. Why are they doing that? Because they sincerely want to end suffering, they want to live a life of compassion. What are you not going to like about such a person? We don't socialize, so we don't have to worry about social skills, or being one-up on each other, or feeling insecure about anything. All of that is very helpful, I think.

Melinda: What we do see about each other is in these discussions, where everybody brings their intimate self and lays it out in the context of this spiritual practice: what we are struggling with, what is hard, what we're learning.

Phyllis: And the content of what we go through doesn't matter; it's the sincerity that makes the connection between us.

Cheri: Because whatever is the most difficult thing in our lives is being faced here.

A.: At our talk before the interviews, when it was mentioned that we might be asked about working with the teacher, I thought, "Well, I hardly ever see her, but I'll go along with the program." I asked Sara if Cheri suggested that question, and if Cheri gave the impression that she was here a lot and we saw her a lot [laughter, especially from Cheri]. But Sara said no, that Cheri had said she wasn't here much at all. That enabled me to see that we look to Phyl as a teacher, we look to Cameron as a teacher when she leads, we look to each other. I even felt that I was in a dharma talk with Sara, and that became guidance for me. It seems that we're all teachers, that the teaching itself is just in the air around here. It's not like, if Cheri's gone and Phyl's gone and Cameron's gone, the rest of us all party down in the dining room.

Cheri: I'm so relieved to hear that.

Cameron: One time I was lamenting that I hadn't seen Cheri in a long time and needed to see her more often. And she told me that she is the guide, not the sherpa [laughter]. In fact, I learn so much from everybody. The training that's going on here is awesome. I'm very grateful to all of you.

Cheri: And to yourself for being able to recognize it. There's a famous quotation about that that is escaping me at the moment. The second line is, "Everything enlightens me." How could each moment not enlighten us if we are present to it? Once we give up our feverish desire to escape from it, once we plunge into the moment and realize that we have no choice other than intimacy with all that is, then everything enlightens us—every thought, every feeling, every bit of resistance, every moment of enthusiasm, of excitement, of memory, of hope—it all enlightens us.

◇

Melinda

Melinda began meditating with the Zen Center and attending retreats at the Monastery in the mid-1980s. A few years ago, when she was in her early fifties, a close friend who was five years younger was diagnosed with cancer at the beginning of August and died by the end of the month. Melinda began to think about going to the Monastery; in response, she figured, to the sudden realization that we do not know what is going to happen. "My friend was not expecting to die; she was still learning how to live. The question for me was, why am I not taking advantage of the best opportunity I have to live as fully as possible?" By the end of the year, Melinda had left her practice as a psychotherapist and joined the community of monks.

1996

Phyl is my teacher now. Cheri is an occasional, almost always wonderful guide. But day to day, most of the ongoing stuff happens with Phyl. She has a deep level of understanding; it may not be as crisp as Cheri's, but she's very well grounded. I may not like some of the things she does—it's happened any number of times that I've gotten enraged—but sooner or later I can see that she is guiding me on my path, with compassion.

I wasn't prepared for what I've come up against within myself. I had no idea how invested I can be in knowing answers and doing things right. I was raised to be a thinker, and there always has been so much reward for me in figuring things out and having knowledge. But the training here shows me how the attachment to thinking and having answers gets in the way of a deeper way of being who I am, a deeper way of knowing. I've learned that thinking doesn't work for me the way I always thought it did. Before, it seemed that I would feel a need to know something, I would go and get an answer, then

I could relax. From a different perspective, what happens is, I feel
the need to know, I go and get a fix, and the habit is reinforced. I
love bird-watching; I see a new bird, I look it up in my bird book,
I find it, and—aah. Not that there's anything wrong with that in
itself; it's just that those pleasures deepen the ruts of my conditioned
idea that having that answer means I am in control. Which, of course,
is a total illusion.

Phyl wanted me to see that things I viewed as positive about
being able to think were in fact barriers to being truly present. Her
guidance switched my way of looking at intelligence, at the thought
process, and helped me get on a clearer track spiritually. I said to Phyl
once, "Do you mean we have to give up pleasure in order to
experience joy?" And she said yes. The pleasure of, "Ah, I know that
bird," or, "Ah, I just figured out who's coming this weekend by the
numbers on the menu," the little explosion of pleasure when you
fit things together—that pleasure keeps me hooked into wanting to
know, keeps me up in my head, robs me of the experience of staying
with my heart. It's the pleasure of, "Got it! I knew I was right" as
opposed to the joy of, "Ah, I have it all. I'm here, present to everything."
You can't have them both, at least not simultaneously.

Getting enraged happens more often with Phyl because I interact
with her day to day, but I also have been really upset with Cheri. A
long time ago, on the way to a retreat here, I was feeling stuck and
wishing for something major to shake me up. When I signed up for
guidance, I was disappointed to see that the time allotted was
shorter than usual; it had been a long time since I'd spoken with
Cheri, and I was really looking forward to it, and also I had some
books I wanted to give her. At the beginning of the guidance
appointment, I gave her the books, and she started looking at them.
I said, "You can look at them later. I want to do my guidance now."
And she said, "The guide does not like to be rushed." I felt that I
had committed a ghastly wrong. I was humiliated, I could barely

keep from crying, I was just holding on. When I left the guidance appointment, I raged and raged, then cried tears and tears and tears. The insight I had from that was about my not being aware of how much I wanted to control the situation, and it was one of those world-opening-up experiences. I was so grateful to her for having reined me in, having shaken me up in that way so I could see that in myself. Later, she said it had been hard for her, that it's always hard for her to do something she knows the other person will experience as wounding. But she has to do it, because that is what we need from her. It is truly the most compassionate thing to do.

◇

I've had a variety of jobs since I've been here. For a while, I was cook, then I was meal planner and shopper. Now I lay tile all day. Very different from being a therapist! Before we moved into the dining room, the expansion joints in the floor had to be caulked, and I did that for a long time. It turned out that the caulk was not quite the right color, so we're going to dig out all of the caulk and lay the tile again.

In addition to the regular rotating jobs, we have other assignments. This week I'm meditation guide, and last week I was kitchen floor mopper, and my permanent jobs are cleaning two outhouses and the utility room and watering a tree. The schedule now is that every day except Wednesday and Sunday, meditation is two half-hour sittings in the morning and two in the evening, when we also have fifteen minutes of walking meditation, and we work from 8:45 to 12:15 and from 1:30 to 4:30. After the second morning sitting, we get our assignments off the message board. Mine this morning said I would be making jam. Yesterday morning it was to work on the tile, and yesterday afternoon it was to work on the tile and write up a description of how to clean the refrigerator. Each morning and each afternoon there's a note, and we never know what our next assignment will be.

One afternoon around three weeks ago there was a note that Russ and I would be leaving at 7:40 the next morning for the Bay Area to do some painting at the Zen Center. The notes are very specific: Russ would drive down, I would drive back, we would have an early breakfast and take a lunch, and when we got down there, we would find out where we would be staying. I hate it and I love it—not knowing, not having control. There are times when I go to get my note, and I'm sure I know what I'm going to be doing, and it says something different and I'm upset. But I've come to appreciate how not knowing is a great relief for some part of me, not *needing* to know, feeling safe with whatever happens rather than false security based on the illusion of control.

People can come here and work for a long time on some issue and feel as if nothing is changing. But Cheri or Phyl or anyone else who's watching can see that they are being transformed. I was backing up the truck one day and hit the fence. Right away, I heard the defensive voice in me saying, "I just don't do things like that! I'm a good driver!" And that was followed by a fearful voice, "Everybody's going to see this terrible thing I've done." At the same time, I realized that although those old tapes were playing, there was no real emotional charge in it. A little bit of some part of myself was saying that I should be ashamed, but in fact I just watched all that going on, with interest, because that whole system wasn't working any more. I actually was not ashamed.

This practice is filled with compassion. I know that even if Phyl does something that seems off the wall, her intention is to help me move a little further along the path. Same with Cheri. They both, ceaselessly, do the practice themselves, and it shows—there is such honesty in them, such sincerity, and they are completely devoted to helping us find the way. The way the training is arranged here, for example: as we are often reminded, it's not about getting the job done, it's about your spiritual practice. It doesn't matter whether that

shower gets tiled or not. What matters is, am I getting the best spiritual training I can get?

If I am told to do something I don't like, I can either get caught up in not liking it and wondering why they're doing this to me, and so on, or I can ask, "How is this part of my training?" The willingness to do that builds on the faith of long experience. Every time I have an experience of opening, there's more faith next time that it's possible. The dark nights of the soul become less tormenting the more one's faith grows. Even when I'm going through something that makes me so angry I could spit nails, I know there's something good on the other side.

1998

For a while I believed that this was like spiritual boot camp, and the idea was to break the will. The whole way the guidelines were set up, the way work is arranged, the way notes are written—all that seemed designed to give ego such a boot that it would surrender. In fact, that is not the case, but it took me a long time to understand that.

For instance, one day I noticed that the person who was in charge of putting supper into the oven had forgotten to do it. My thought was, "I guess he'll get a note about this and have to face the embarrassment of having it pointed out to him that he was not paying attention." But when I told Phyl about it, she said, "Why didn't you put it in the oven yourself?" Well—hmmm. That was interesting, because I saw two things. One is that everything that is humanly possible is done here to *not* have us feel bad about ourselves. The point of a note is *not* to humiliate anybody, but to guide us back to center when we've strayed off course and don't seem to be aware of it. The monk who forgot to put the meal in the oven probably did not get a note about it, because he would be aware of what happened as soon as the meal was served—cold. The second thing is that, being off center myself, when I saw the other person's oversight, I did nothing to correct it, which contributed to everybody having to eat a cold meal. In this case, compassion—or nonseparateness—might have been best expressed in a common sense action that overrides a guideline like, "It's the other person's job, so I'd better not get involved."

The idea is not so much to bump us up against ego at its most awful as to love it to death, to be so compassionate that ego doesn't need to run our lives any more. That was such a shift for me, to go from, "They're trying to break my will" to "They're supporting my transformation."

This practice assists people in finding their own strength, their own ability to be perfectly okay, rather than fostering a dependence on someone who knows how they should be and can teach them. This means learning to find that clarity inside that enables us to respond appropriately in each moment. There are circumstances when I'm much more likely to do that, such as being in the role of facilitator. All of us are being trained as workshop facilitators, so we all have the experience of setting aside our need for control enough to be fully present with someone, to hear what they're saying, to assist them to find their own response, rather than trying to help, which usually comes from our own conditioning. Ultimately, the reason we do facilitator training is to learn how we can offer that same quality of presence and listening and compassionate acceptance within ourselves. If I should ever return to working as a therapist, I think it would be very different, in that I would do whatever I could to have people not be dependent, to get them beyond the assumption that I was doing something that they couldn't do for themselves. That's something Cheri is so rigorous about. And it's so helpful for us to be constantly turned back to that.

Recently, I have been seeing the movement of my attention away from the present as up and out, and when my attention is here, with my heart, it's down and in. If my attention moves to my thoughts, then I'm out somewhere else. If my attention is with my breath, down in the center, then I can stay at home. The other day I saw a bird I didn't recognize, and my impulse was to look it up. But then I saw that that would be another point for ego: looking it up separates me from the bird and makes it an "it," so there's a subject-object division; that's what the up and out movement does. Whereas the down and in is—spaciousness. Absence of clutter. More and more I experience what goes on up here, in the head, as clutter. When I'm able to stay at home, there's all the room in the world; in that spaciousness, anything can arise, and it will be all right.

My experience was that being in the world was not intense enough, that on my own I did not have the willingness to seriously challenge egocentricity. When I'm out in the world now on occasion, I will turn on the radio and listen to the news or check out the headlines, and I see that the pull of the things that kept me from being able to go completely inward hasn't lost its force. Being in the Monastery simply makes it so much easier to pursue what really matters to me.

Making the transition from my life outside to my life here was so easy. There were no second thoughts, and haven't been, in three years and a month. I am the only person I have never heard say, "I've had times when I wanted to leave." From my first months here, it was completely clear that I have everything I want.

3

Silence

In the dining hall, tall, rough-hewn shelves are labeled with first names of the monks and guests to mark places for storing a dinner plate, small plate, bowl, mug, and silverware for each person. One of the more obvious guidelines is to use only your own dining utensils and wash them and return them to their place on the shelves after each meal.

Simple enough. Yet in an unfamiliar situation, without asking questions about how things are done and receiving reassurance from others, you can feel vulnerable. And in addition to not speaking at the Monastery, you don't look around and observe what others are doing. Not looking at people is an important guideline in supporting the "privileged environment"; it is part of the practice, a visual silence. Thus is the stage set for internal melodramas of the type I call "ego catastrophe."

When I first approached the dining hall shelves, it was with a certain awe. Each nested set of stoneware dishes (given by a potter who made them for the Monastery) is like a still-life composition, repeated, with slight variations in shapes and colors, at exact intervals on the grid of plank shelving: an arrangement of pure elegance, approaching perfection. Extricating one's plate and mug, say, or small plate and bowl from the stacked set can be a challenge. It needs to be accomplished quickly so as not to hold up those waiting to get theirs and also carefully so as to avoid dropping something, a blunder greatly intensified when you are in silence. I was grateful that my name was in the middle, not on the top shelf or the bottom, which would have added a degree of difficulty. Each mealtime, I approached those shelves intent on mindfully retrieving my dishes in a way that would reflect some modest degree of spiritual attainment, especially in case my actions were inadvertently (or surreptitiously) observed.

After several days, alertness waning, I came in a few minutes early and took down the mug for a cup of tea. As I filled it with steaming water, I noticed that it didn't feel quite right in my hand. It didn't look right, either. I glanced back at the shelves and saw my mug still in its place—and no mug at Melinda's place, next to mine.

At that moment, Melinda began bringing in platters of food. I dashed into the kitchen, poured out the hot tea, rinsed the mug, and put it back over her name. As I picked up my own mug and felt the chill of its surface, I realized that Melinda might notice the warmth of her mug, and—what?

Ego catastrophe! The double guilt of not only making a mistake but trying to cover it up, wanting to be (or at least be seen as) good, right, perfect—a common, garden-variety but nonetheless tormenting source of suffering.

I didn't look at Melinda, but I saw her in my mind's eye and asked myself, what would she do when she picked up her unexpectedly warm mug? Because we are at the Monastery, most likely she will do nothing. I don't apologize, she doesn't reassure; within the silence, each of us accepts full responsibility for herself.

"But what if . . .?" ego whispers. "What if she realizes I am the culprit, will she think ill of me?" Probably not. The monks' training is to refrain from speculating or otherwise concerning themselves about what may be going on with others—an important and much-valued aspect of the silence.

My guess is that even if Melinda came to get her dinnerware and all of it was gone, she would meet the challenge with some quick creative thinking. In any case, I could leave her to deal with her experience in the faith that she is inherently capable of doing so. That is the deal; that is the respect people offer each other within the all-embracing silence, the habit of nonreactivity that provides the uniquely safe privileged environment.

So, was there a catastrophe? I imagined discussing the incident with Melinda and could see her pointing out that what I did was the only sensible thing: I rinsed the cup and put it back. If Melinda noticed its warmth, either she would realize what had happened, and might even find it amusing, or she would go right on living with a bit of mystery woven into the abounding mysteries discovered and cherished in a life of silence.

◇

Tony

Growing up in a devout Catholic family, Tony considered becoming a priest. He attended seminary for two years and spent time at a Benedictine monastery, but eventually decided to marry. In 1989, Tony got a teaching job in Malaysia, and for two years he and his wife lived and traveled extensively in Southeast Asia. Back in this country, friends they had known in Asia had discovered the Monastery, which is near where they live. When Tony and his wife came to visit, their friends had signed them up for a retreat.

My first exposure to Zen was a work retreat at the Monastery, and it didn't appeal to me much. My interest was in learning to meditate. When we found out that a *sesshin* [intensive meditation period] was scheduled in the next week or so, I thought that would be a good opportunity to learn more about meditation, so I signed up. That was a totally different experience from a work retreat, and it made me eager to find out more. So, I signed up for two more retreats. By then I was hooked and wanted to spend more time here. I asked if that was possible, and was told yes. So, my wife and I drove back to the Midwest and tied up some loose ends, and I came back here for a more extended stay. Linda practices a Southeast Asian form of Buddhism, so while I was at the Monastery she took the time to go back overseas and study with her teacher.

I didn't know what to expect when I came here for the first stay, except that I expected something really, really different. It was. Of course, there's silence all the time, and work, and time alone. The schedule was different then; there was a lot of unscheduled time, and I didn't know what to do with that. It was a chance to look at a lot of things about myself, about my past life, about what I thought I was moving toward, all those sorts of things that people like to ponder. Mostly, it was learning a new way of—I was going to say "thinking," but it's more than that: it's a new way of being, or being a new way with yourself. For me, the inevitable consequence is that you're being a new way with everyone, everything, all beings, all of the created order. In the searching I had done before, the new perspectives and knowledge I acquired were added onto what was already there. There was a sense of broadening, certainly, that naturally leads to growth and compassion and other things like that. But for me, Zen has been a shift at such a basic level that nothing else I've ever done can compare with it.

The main things I got out of that first stay here were the tools to do the practice and the beginnings of a commitment to the practice. When I left the Monastery after seven months, it happened that Linda arrived back from her trip overseas on the same day. So, we returned to the Midwest together. That was my first chance to apply the practice outside. I was in a state of sensory overload after being here for so long. Things were still fantastic in a lot of ways, as if I were seeing things for the first time and not yet knowing what to do with that. Everything was filled with meaning, like having an understanding of what words like "compassion" really mean. It was very much what you'd call a religious experience. Everything felt very special. I remember trying to explain some of this when we were home, and I couldn't explain it then any more than I can now.

It was clear that I wanted to come back here, because I knew I was just beginning something. I'm in an enviable position in that I have the time to do this and a wife who is willing for me to do this while she is doing her thing.

When I came back here for a second stay, I got down to the process of just practicing. Maybe it was getting acclimated to a new way of seeing, a new way of paying attention, but things returned to a more normal state in that I was just here doing whatever I was doing. Brushing my teeth was no longer the totally, even ridiculously magical thing it was for a while; it was just brushing my teeth. That's not to say it is the same as before I started this practice. There is a different sense of attention, a sense of mystery, moment by moment, but that's what is normal now.

In retrospect, I see that I didn't know what I was getting into, I had only a foggy grasp of what was to come. The second stay started out well. I had been going through a blissful period, feeling good about everything, then all at once, I knew that wasn't enough. I got shocked out of my complacency by a series of events—I don't know how to describe this. Cameron talks about the "wrecking ball of life," which means that just when you think you're getting this Zen stuff, something happens and you realize you haven't gotten anything at all, or what you got wasn't straight. I suppose what it amounts to is that you achieve a new insight, then you realize all at once that what you had known before wasn't the full picture. I had been understanding a lot of stuff only with my head, and it hadn't penetrated down to my heart. I knew the words, but I hadn't experienced it yet. It was very hard to see that. Cheri was there to talk me through it. She was very helpful, and as painful as the experience was, I was grateful for it.

After that, I began to have deeper experiences. In the spring, I went into a really black place. Just—[pause] really tough. It was complete resistance to the practice. At the same time, I was experiencing an immense amount of joy and clarity. A lot of times the resistance seems to come as a consequence of the freedom; I was starting to experience some freedom, then there was what seemed like a backlash, which was as horrible as the freedom had been wonderful.

For example: it's a beautiful Sunday afternoon, I have some free hours, and I walk down to the creek. I turn a bend and there's this panoramic landscape, the sun is shining, the birds are singing, it's a warm spring day—just go through the list, everything is wonderful. I'm really feeling good, totally present (at least, as present as I could be at that time), and everything is filled with a sense of wonder and awe. By the time I get to the bottom of the hill in ten or fifteen minutes, I'm in a place of horror. I remember walking back up that hill feeling as if I were pulling a car behind me, in such a state of misery that thoughts went through the mind like, "Why not just end it? Here's a steep cliff, just walk off."

Fortunately, we talk about how this kind of experience can happen when you're doing a practice like this, how you can go from one state to another so quickly, so I had been aware of the possibility of that before it actually occurred. That helped me stay present enough in the awfulness of it to remember that I was at the same bend in the road where I'd been standing twenty minutes before. Then, all had been bliss, and now voices in my head were saying, "I can't stand it," that they'd rather I die than go on.

In that moment, it was helpful to recall Cheri and others saying that ego doesn't want you to do this practice; it made it possible for me to have the awareness that this was a passing phase, this was just ego: "Ah, ha, this is ego talking to me right now. Ego doesn't care what happens to me; in fact, right now it's hoping that something bad happens to me."

I went through maybe a month of that kind of stuff. I didn't know if I'd get through from day to day, I didn't know if I'd manage to stay here at the Monastery or not. Many times I wanted to get in my car and leave. And I didn't. I don't know why. I'm very grateful that I didn't, because I know that if I had left then, that would have been as far as I ever would have gotten in this practice. If I had lost nerve climbing that particular very steep hill, I would never have had the nerve to tackle it again. But I made it through, and by April, certainly by May, I was experiencing the freedom I'd been feeling back in March, but without all the muck coming up in response.

About that period, about how hard it can be at the Monastery—in a way, I'm hesitant to talk about it. I wouldn't want to scare people

off by suggesting that they may end up facing something really awful. They may not have that experience. What I was facing I brought with me, so to speak; someone else would be facing whatever it is that they carry around with them in their own lives.

Finally, from the vantage point of having already gone through some difficult places, I find there is a part of me that is eager to face it again. It's kind of like mountain climbing: it's when the going is the steepest that there is the best chance for real upward movement. And, ohhh—the view when you get to the top! Then you know the effort was worth it. It isn't possible to say how grateful I am for this experience.

$$\diamond$$

I've pondered the role of the guide [Cheri]. I have the sense that the guide is the person who gives me permission to be doing spiritual practice, who tells me that it's appropriate for me to be doing this. Part of me is grateful for that, and part of me is afraid of that. It's a classic sort of love-hate relationship. The part of me who really wants to do this practice is the part who's had me searching all over the world for something. The part of me that does not want to be doing this practice sees it as terribly threatening. As the person who represents the practice, Cheri gets all this stuff projected onto her. So, I find myself looking forward to being around her, and at the same time, it's never a clean or pure feeling; there's always fear as well. The fear, I suppose, is the part of me that is afraid of what I'm going to do. And since she represents that, there's both gratitude and eagerness to be with her, to hear what she's going to say, to be in guidance appointments, all of that, but there's also anxiety about where it's going to lead to next.

During that period when things were so tough, I remember being resentful that I was going through that totally alone for several weeks. Then Cheri showed up and I had a guidance appointment. I recall that we did not say much at all, that she was very silent. She just sat with me. But I came away with—with what was needed to keep going on. Without her speaking any words, what I heard was, this is something you have to get through, no one can do it for you; I'll do everything I can to help, but you've got to do it yourself.

So, I see how helpful it can be that Cheri is not always here. I don't know if that is by design or not. The result is that I am forced to be my own guide, to rely on my own inner wisdom, to find my own way. And I did get through that dark period on my own. I suppose it's inevitable that I will go through dark periods in the future, and now I have the experience, if and when they arise, that yes, I can do this tough stuff. I don't need to lean on anyone.

$\Diamond$

After my second stay at the Monastery, I went home to visit family and friends. While I was there, I attempted to do my own *sesshin,* camping in the woods near my parents' home. I found it very difficult to meditate alone for six days. The first time I tried, I sat for three days, and then something came up, so I quit. Then I tried again and sat two or three days, and something else came up. After this pattern repeated several times, it became clear that even though I had tried to set up my own little privileged environment, there was nothing guarding it, nothing guaranteeing it to the same degree that is true at the Monastery. So, while the things that came up were not really urgent, three days into a *sesshin,* which is usually when most of my resistance is right there in my face, it was all too easy to find something else to do. I saw what was happening, and eventually I just sat through the whole six days. It was a helpful experience, because it got me to see resistance and to watch the process of backing down in the face of resistance several times before I went all the way through the full six days. At the end of that six days, I went on a binge of not paying attention—reading until I fell asleep sitting upright, engaging my family in discussions—all the things I could grab to take me out of the moment, to dissipate the energy, the awareness that was the consequence of the sitting. It was also good to see that dissipation process.

For the most part, I've been in a good place for the last several months. I've seen a lot of resistance to the practice, but that alternates with a lot of openness, a lot of willingness to do the practice. I can see what's going on, I have a lot of things that clue me in on it, and I'm comfortable with that pattern now.

Like today, the resisting comes in not being able to pay attention, at least not the way I was able to earlier this week. If I weren't aware of this, I would be cranky today, in a foul mood, feeling that everything is wrong. But I see that what's happening is just that I'm being resistant. It's tempting to focus on why I don't feel good the way I did earlier this week, but more and more I am able to say, well, I'm being resistant today; there'll be a lot to look at, and this will be a great opportunity to practice. So, what could have been a bad experience, if I weren't paying attention, becomes an opportunity to come back to the present repeatedly throughout the day. In fact, it becomes a superb day in that I get to practice over and over and over again coming back to the present, and I get to experience how bringing my attention back feels so much better than being off somewhere else. It's really wonderful to be able to welcome the resistance in a way that defuses it. I accept this as a day with a different energy, a different way of being aware.

◇

I've been seeking all my life to discover what it means to be a creature—that is, someone created by God. Coming to Zen was originally for me more an intellectual experience; that is, I was going to study the philosophy of Zen, not the religion of Zen. Now it seems to me that this was what I was searching for the whole

time and just didn't know it. Which, I guess, is Zen—the process
of being totally aware of what's going on, although that doesn't mean
there are any answers. For a long time I was searching for answers,
and now I'm more comfortable with there just being questions.

For me, Zen is the practice of living one's life from the deepest
meaning possible. It is a way of being, so it is deeply religious in one
sense. But Zen is not about beliefs; it's process rather than content.
Zen is a way of *being* your religion, and that's what I practice Zen for.

Mystics are not people who are easily controlled, and my suspicion
is that in the Church hierarchy, there has been a deliberate down-
playing of the mystical side of Christianity, in the interest of keeping
things safe and orderly and under control. For me, a lot of the difficulty
with religion is how it becomes encumbered with society's teachings,
so when you learn a religion, along with it, you get society's values
and judgments; society interprets the religion. Now I have something
else with which to interpret my Christianity, which is Zen. At some
point, I began seeing how all the things Jesus said were the things
a Zen master would say. That is, Zen made it possible for me to see
in a different light what Jesus was trying to communicate. And that
has had a very powerful effect in deepening my Christian faith.

Solitude

Solitude allows us to be with ourselves in a way that is rarely possible in ordinary circumstances. It is hard to get to know ourselves when we are constantly looking to others to gain approval and assign blame; those are ways of establishing our distinctness without gaining any self-knowledge. Only when we look inward do we discover that we have what it takes to feel completely at home in the world, that we already are everything we need, that the sense of separation between us and the rest of existence is an illusion, with sad and destructive consequences. Thus, the paradox: to discover our connectedness, we must first be alone with ourselves.

"Liberation is not a group activity," Cheri points out, which makes it hard to pursue in regular life. "That's why there are monasteries. There always have been places for people who want to do spiritual practice in an environment that makes it a little bit easier." In the following excerpt from a talk, Cheri discusses the shift from a sense of separate identity that is continually reinforced by social interaction—and the concomitant fear of being alone—to the experience of infinite connection with all of existence.

> When people first encounter our practice, two things that strike them as strange are the silence and the lack of eye contact. They ask, "How do you ever get to know anybody, or feel close to anybody?" But once they have gone through

a ten-day retreat, they are in love with the other retreatants, they think this is the most extraordinary group of people they've ever met, they want to live together the rest of their lives, and they don't even know one another's names. So often, the opposite experience—engaging with people in normal social situations—actually has the effect of creating distance between individuals; certainly it tends to separate us from ourselves. The usual social chit-chat is not that different, in function or in purpose, from watching television: it distracts us from paying attention to what is going on inside us.

This is not to say that silence is always superior to interaction. The key is the degree of urgency in our need to interact. Until we prove to ourselves that we can be all right with or without talking, we're not free, because there's that underlying fear: "What if I feel I really need to connect with somebody, and there's nobody there?" We often stay in situations we don't like—a job, a relationship—because we're afraid of not having it. We will endure being with somebody we don't really want to be with just so if the day comes when we don't want to be alone, we can fall back on the safety of that relationship. But once we prove to ourselves that we are all right with it and we are all right without it, then there's the freedom to connect with somebody when it's time to do that, and to be alone when it's time to do that.

I never met anyone who was drawn to this kind of spiritual practice who didn't eventually prefer the life of silence to ordinary social life. What I mean is this: if one had to choose always to be in the company of others or always to be alone, most people who have done monastic training would choose the latter. Because, of course, the whole trick of spiritual practice is to realize that *we are not alone.*

◇

Shonen

Shonen is an American woman who has lived for thirteen years at a Zen monastery in Japan, where she was ordained as a Buddhist nun. She attended a workshop and spent a month at the Monastery in 1997 and is currently there for a longer stay. In this interview, Shonen describes how her spiritual practice has given her a more compassionate under-standing of herself as a blind person.

I came to Zen Buddhist practice when I was thirty. I was seeking, at an especially difficult time in my life, a person who could teach me about the truth, about inherent goodness, about how to live without suffering, and about how to help other people live without suffering. I had spent most of my life trying to figure things out analytically through thinking, and that had never worked; I was still suffering terribly. I thought Zen would offer a different way of looking into things. Also, in Zen there are teachers, people who through their own experience had understood True Nature and were teaching that and could teach me, which I had never found in my experience of Christianity.

I realized not only that I could not do this alone and that I needed the help of a teacher, but also that I needed to do it full-time. I didn't know of any place in the United States where that was possible, but I thought there must be opportunities in Japan since most of the books I'd read were written by people who had trained there. So I went to Japan to live in a monastery.

My teacher there is wonderful, a man of deep insight. He had a very traditional Japanese Zen training, but he is quite extraordinary in several ways. He is vegetarian, which is unusual in Japan, and he is a celibate, which is rare; the Japanese priests mostly have families. Also, he allows women and foreigners to train in his temple and has always given them an equal place. Various people thought that because I am blind I should not be allowed to be a monk, but he made it possible for someone like me with great difficulties to be there and to train. I project that that is because his own faith in the teachings of the Buddha is so great that he's been able to stay in that truth himself and be a support for many other people who are not understanding that.

In fact, I feel that he saved my life. In the twelve years I have practiced with him, I went through phases of the deepest despair, suicidal feelings and desperation and panic and anger and fear of immense proportions, terrified over nothing, at least nothing that was apparent externally. I would be so physically overwhelmed that I would not be able to function for hours and days. Through all that he supported me and had faith in me. In my darkest hours, he showed me great compassion, and that compassion has been like a shining beacon for me. It kept me alive through a time that I might not have survived if I'd been alone.

I discovered this particular practice through tapes of Cheri's books, particularly *There Is Nothing Wrong With You*. Probably the main difficulty in my life up to that point in Zen practice was feeling so much hate and fear of myself. I felt that I could have love for other people and compassion for them and even compassion for my suffering, but I still feared and hated myself because I hadn't understood the inherent goodness of life. The perspective of that book was a significant help to me in seeing what was really causing my difficulties.

I came to this Monastery at a point in my practice when I wasn't getting anywhere, thinking that I would like to do a retreat alone. I did not know that it would be totally silent here. Because I'm blind, when I arrived and found that I couldn't get information through hearing, I was quite frightened. I actually got sick and stayed in bed during the first evening workshop. The next afternoon I did the same thing, which was something that had happened to me for many years—I would get so overwhelmed by self-hate that I wouldn't be able to function. One of the monks came to my dorm room and said, "You cannot do this here. You have to participate in every activity." I felt that I was going to die if I had to get out of bed and go to the dining hall that evening. But somehow I did it. And I've never had that problem at the Monastery since then. This is the first time in fifteen years that I've been able to function every day without becoming so depressed that I would have to go to my room and lie down and shut myself in for hours and days at a time.

During that first month here I had another experience that was very interesting. Having had difficulty with my eyes since birth, I had always believed that my problems are caused by my blindness: that I was inferior to other people, that I was not able to function like other people, that I was not considered good enough by other people, and many other self-hating beliefs that I had about myself that I had always connected with the fact that I can't see. But during that workshop I had a very clear insight that even if I had been able to see perfectly, my experience of life and how people treat me would be exactly the same as long as I believed that I should be different. I could have been a person with whatever admirable qualities—the most beautiful, most intelligent, most vivacious, physically agile and artistically talented—and, given the same conditioning from my parents and my social environment, I still would have experienced that sense of inadequacy.

That was a powerful moment when I understood that each one of us has a story or a reason why we feel inadequate. Being blind was my reason; that was what everything got pinned on from infancy, that I couldn't see. Actually, the real reason is the same for everybody: the human condition of separation and fear and hatred. Now I realize that I had many beliefs about myself and other people that I attributed to being blind but that are simply self-hating beliefs and have nothing to do with the fact that I don't see.

The space of silence and solitude at the Monastery is rare in this world and can be valuable for anyone, as a way to be with themselves and deepen their understanding of themselves. The compassionate support of the other people here and the structure of the Monastery schedule enable me to practice within the silence and solitude in a more effective way. I've felt more support here than I've felt in my entire life, because everyone around me is taking responsibility for their own thoughts and their own beliefs about the world and not (at least verbally) projecting that on me. The teaching of compassion at the Monastery, which is so pervasive, includes the aspect of adequacy, that each individual is completely adequate to their own life and adequate to be compassionate for themselves. That has enabled me to begin to give up that fear of myself and that hate of myself and see it for what it is, the illusion that arises from egocentricity.

I have found group discussion to be really helpful. It shows that everyone has the same thoughts, the same problems. There are individual versions, but they come down to the same root: the experience of fear and hatred. To see that everyone has the same experience is helpful in two ways. First, all of us feel that we're more hopeless than anyone else, and in the other direction, to balance that out, we often feel that we're more special than anyone else, that we have more and better insights than anyone else. But when we sit in a group and hear what other people have to say about their suffering, we learn that they have very similar experiences of it, and we also see that other people have amazing insights into their lives. Second, the process of being in the group and hearing other people's experiences evokes compassion that we may not feel for ourselves. But in hearing about someone else's suffering and in feeling that compassion, you experience it within yourself. It's really helpful to get an actual bodily, emotional, intellectual, total experience of that compassion so that we can find that for ourselves as well as for other people.

Now I realize that I began sitting [meditation] to get rid of my painful thinking, which seemed to be causing me suffering. I sat in order to get to some better state, enlightenment or clarity; I sat in order to be a good person. I sat to get approval from my teacher, thinking that if I did good, clear sitting he would approve of me and I would be loved. So I was always going in opposite directions, pushing away the hate and fear in my mind in order to get what I needed from outside. As I have been able to get some distance on all this, I've seen self-hate as being an illusion, not being who I truly am. I am beginning to be drawn toward the goodness within myself, to love and nurture it, and that seems to me to be what meditation is about. In sitting itself, in paying attention to the breath and counting each breath, what I am actually doing is being with myself and loving myself. And sitting in order to enjoy that experience of love makes it something I want to do, something I enjoy rather than a torture or a discipline.

It's very exciting to come upon a teacher like Cheri Huber because she exemplifies to me the living teachings of the Buddha. What she has to say seems always to be fresh and inspiring. The clarity with which she expresses the teachings in simple, ordinary language makes it totally accessible and understandable to anyone. There's no need to have any special knowledge or education or experience with Buddhist terminology or foreign culture. She expresses that living truth directly in her own way, not relying on how people have said or done things in the past.

Cheri's depth of insight and the way that (in my perception) she lives from True Nature in a moment to moment way is an indication that Americans, ordinary Westerners, human beings who have grown up in this day and age and society, can reach that original goodness that we all feel somehow and that we all know must be there. I've been extraordinarily happy to meet her and to hear what she has to say, because her perspective on practice seems to me to be in the strictest sense totally in line with what the Buddha was teaching, from what I understand of it. That perspective is very different from almost every other perspective in our society. It's so unusual because it's so broad, it includes everything, it isn't against anything. I think that anyone who can listen to the perspective Cheri offers will find it quite mind-expanding and heart-opening. It can give everyone more ways to explore how, within their total life and environment and experience, to learn to be with what is. The point is that an ordinary American growing up in our society today is living the same truth, with the same heart and mind as the Buddha did 2,500 years ago—that that is possible, that it happens right here, with us.

Only One Rule

At the Monastery, in addition to the general guidelines listed in the last section of this book, there are specific guidelines for all the activities that take place—meditation, working, eating, cleaning up, maintenance, and so on—as well as guidelines for being in the kitchen, dining hall, dormitory, hermitages, and even the outdoors. These are not to be understood as fixed rules, which would be antithetical to Buddhist teaching. First of all, Buddhist teaching is based on the impermanence of all experience, and guidelines may change in response to changing situations. Also, one's relationship to guidelines changes.

Whereas a rule limits possibilities, a guideline asks that we be aware. For example, the guideline to stay on established paths and roads provides an opportunity to examine all sorts of conditioning when the impulse arises to cut across a field or tramp through the brush. It can bring us face to face with the values we attach to "personal freedom" and our reaction to feeling deprived of it. It can illuminate our relationship to authority, both external and internal. It can challenge us to distinguish conditioned mind from a direct response to present-moment experience.

Other aspects of how guidelines work in spiritual training are described in the following excerpt from one of Cheri's talks.

To people coming to the Monastery for the first time, it can seem as if we have an awful lot of rules. We say we have many guidelines, but only one rule: to use everything in our experience to see how we cause ourselves to suffer so that we can stop doing those things and end suffering. The rest are merely guidelines, which position us to see more clearly what our conditioning is and how it causes suffering. That *seeing* is the whole point of a place like this.

In fact, all of us have unstated rules about the way things are done in our own living space; we just aren't aware of them. A quick check on the truth of that is to move in with somebody. So, at the Monastery, rather than dropping people into a silent environment with no orientation, to me it seems kind to let people know how we do things here. That is also what the guidelines are for.

Most of the guidelines are based in the first precept, not to live a harmful life. Now, most of us are conditioned to consider "harm" only in relation to other human beings; if it doesn't harm another person, it's probably all right. Some of us have extended that to apply to other creatures, all sentient beings. We may even go beyond that and wonder what makes "sentient" such a big deal, who's going to decide what that is? How about—what the heck—all beings? We might even question why we would want to be harmful toward something we don't consider a "being." Why wouldn't we want to bring the same care and attention to all of it— to the rocks, to the walls, to the books, to the dirt, to everything?

For example, everything here was contributed by somebody. Not only did the wood come from the earth, but somebody made a donation to the Zen Center to buy it. Somebody spent a lot of time and energy and effort converting those pieces of redwood into these windows and doors. So, here are these beautiful windowsills, and if there's a rough place on the bottom of a dish, it could scar the wood surface, and when we were moving, people were placing dishes on the windowsills. To me, that lacked respect for the windowsills and for everything it took to have them here.

But the ultimate purpose of the guidelines is that they bring us to the present moment and thus lead us to freedom. In the moment in which we are following a guideline instead of egocentricity, we are released from the bondage of our karmic conditioning from the past. I remember Jennifer talking about being in a difficult situation and what a comfort it was to have the schedule to come back to. Within the structure of the guidelines, we don't have to look to egocentric conditioning to know how to operate. We can simply be guided by what's next on the schedule or how things are done here, and find freedom in that. That is a fundamental aspect of what goes into making the Monastery a privileged environment.

◇

Jeff

Jeff was twenty-eight when he attended his first meditation retreat and met Cheri. Two months later, he moved to the Monastery. Now in his fourth year as a monk, Jeff told in this interview—with much rueful laughter—how he has experimented with setting additional guidelines for himself as a way of moving his practice to a new level.

What I'm left with in this environment is myself. I have a front row seat to watch all my likes, dislikes, fears, attempts to control/manipulate/get my way, and to watch my judgments about myself and others. A huge part of my practice is simply observing all this as it's going on. It's not always fun. And yet, I am experiencing a growing sense of peace in the midst of the suffering, an ability to be with myself compassionately, however I'm feeling, whatever is happening. Every so often, I see through or let go of a pattern of thought or behavior that has caused me misery for a very long time, and I become more alive, more free, more open to life, more joyful, more at peace, and somehow "larger" than I was before. I'm discovering a level of life that is unaffected by the suffering that I am immersed in most of the time. That is also the place from which the suffering can be seen for what it is, accepted, and embraced in compassion. It's that place—my True Nature, my heart—that I'm getting acquainted with and practicing living from.

Recently, I was feeling pretty stuck. I had had a sense for some time that I was not giving as much to the practice as I could; that I was holding back from accepting responsibility, putting my personal comfort ahead of what would be best for all concerned. In a group discussion, someone suggested that a way to get unstuck and to find joy is to be challenged.

Soon after that, I was offered (in my own mind, at least) two challenges by Cheri. One was having her point out that I had not followed instructions in a work assignment. The other was her asking me to speed up something I was doing because I was holding up other people. These incidents, from the outside, seem trivial. But inside I felt threatened, separate from all the other monks who were *really* doing the practice.

In both cases, some part of me knew that I was indulging ego before Cheri pointed it out to me. But in other ways, I was so certain that what I was doing was justified. So, sometimes I need someone else to offer me a larger perspective on what's going on, to call my attention to how what I'm doing affects everybody else. Cheri does that for me. She exposed the narrow focus (ego) I was operating from. And, since I was identified with ego at the time, I didn't like it at all. But to the part of me that wants to do spiritual practice, that wants freedom, joy, and an end to suffering, having these things brought to my attention is a wonderful gift, because once I see what's happening, I can no longer rationalize egocentric actions. If I'm going to continue acting in the same ways, it will be with the knowledge that I'm choosing ego over my heart, maintaining my identity as a separate self.

Again and again, I see that when I choose egocentricity, it's because of fear. A challenge I have set for myself is to confront my fears of physical discomfort. When Cheri mentioned that at the monastery where she trained, the monks got up at 4 a.m. and worked until 8:30 p.m., I thought, if it worked for Cheri, maybe it will work for me. After discussing it with Cheri in guidance, I decided to give it a try. Even though I wasn't clear on why I was doing it, or why it would be helpful, I started working most evenings until 8:30, going to bed at 11, and getting up at 4.

Much of the time, it seemed absolutely crazy. Why in the world would I be doing this? Early on, I was utterly exhausted and could hardly keep my eyes open until 11. Surely, it seemed, the compassionate thing would be to go to bed. But I didn't want to give up and regret it later, so I endured it. And, to my amazement, on some nights when I was exhausted, trying to summon the willingness to keep my eyes open, poof!—suddenly, I would be awake, alive, filled with energy. I can't predict it or make it happen. But the contrast is so stark and the transformation so immediate that there's no denying it.

I also started taking showers in the evenings after finishing work instead of during the day. In winter, it was chilly, and being cold is one of the things I'm most afraid of. I generally dreaded that part of the evening and would start the shower halfway terrified. But, almost always, at some point, just as with the late-night exhaustion, the experience would change. I would be just as cold, but somehow it would not be unbearable, and I would still feel the sensations of fear, but the fear would not have the power over me that it did before.

How does this happen? I don't know. But I have experienced that transformation over and over: I'm afraid, I face the object of my fear, and in the facing of it, I am transformed.

Also, in freeing myself from fear and a belief in my own inadequacy, I free myself from the sense of being a victim or being owed by life, from self-hate, hatred of others, self-centeredness, self-absorption, greed, the need to control. All that stuff seems to come in a single package. If I buy into any one piece, I get all of it. To me, the tremendous suffering that exists in the world—war, hate, the cruel ways we respond to each other in ordinary life, the harsh and unkind ways we treat ourselves—all must arise from the same source, that fearful sense of inadequacy that seems to be at the root of suffering.

I'd prefer to think that being compassionate means "taking care of myself" by keeping myself feeling safe and comfortable, and by avoiding the difficult or challenging parts of life. More often, though, it seems to me that compassion manifests as courage, as willingness, as endurance; and very often it means facing that which I fear, dislike, or believe I can't stand.

It's not that I need to push myself to extremes to prove something. But I think it is important to keep challenging fear and my sense of inadequacy at the edges of where I believe my limits to be. Otherwise, I think, fear has a tendency to eat away at those edges, to make my life smaller and smaller. On the other hand, when I'm willing to risk, to face life as it is, I usually find that, in fact, I am adequate. At that point, fear has nothing to threaten me with. I've already faced what it told me I could not face. And, when I'm not living in fear, when it doesn't seem that my survival is at stake every moment, I have much less need to try to control life, or to do things that cause harm to myself or anyone else. When the fear is not believable, what is left is peace, well-being, an awareness of being alive, and—would you believe it?—joy!

The Unexpected and the All Too Familiar

The monastic path comes complete with unanticipated twists and turns, along with stretches of sameness. High adventure in the mystical realm may or may not develop but is unlikely to take the form expected. Much more predictable is that monks will encounter the very same mundane difficulties that had dogged their lives previously. Just as her own training began with struggles that were utterly familiar, Cheri points out that the daily challenges of the monks she directs are all too human.

When I went into the monastery, I thought everybody there must be holy, so I could go there and be holy, and that would be the end of my problems. And in about six weeks, I had recreated the very life I had lived outside, complete with people I liked and people I hated. So, it is my experience that the monastic setting is exactly like the rest of the world, in that a large part of the difficulties encountered are personality differences. This person thinks that person is picking on him; that person thinks this person has an easier job. It's like having a bunch of children. At our monastery, when Cameron was the work director and Greg was the general contractor on the building, they lived in two different universes, which were on a constant collision course. So, there they were, each trying to be a good monk: watching different aspects of themselves arise in those conflicts, watching what they project onto one another, trying to disidentify from their egocentric conditioning, trying to stay present to each moment, even when things are so hard that they feel they just can't stand it.

People who are living out in the world can follow this same practice. One person is dealing with her reactions to her boss. Another is working with a partner in a relationship. But it's the same process of looking within and questioning everything. What is it about this person that causes this reaction? What are you bringing to the conflict? What are you clinging to? How are you causing yourself to suffer? In each situation, the spiritual guidance would be the same: to watch carefully and bring everything you see into compassionate awareness.

On the other hand, someone who is cultivating ever greater openness to life is likely to encounter ever more that is unexpected. Life in a monastery may seem too circumscribed to permit big surprises, but it's still life, and so it continues to move and change and to have the power to wake us up.

It was certainly unexpected when two of the monks decided to marry each other. Greg, Jennifer, and Phyllis were the first people to enter monastic training. Jennifer and Phyllis had worked together as Montessori teachers when they met Cheri and became part of the Zen Center in Mountain View in the early 1980s. Greg, who was also in that group, was especially eager to acquire land and build a retreat center/monastery. His ambition was clear: to become a Zen monk. After that happened, however, he fell in love with Jennifer. He spoke to Cheri about it over a long period of time, but, being a model monk, did nothing to pursue a relationship. Eventually, Cheri suggested that the only way the issue would be resolved was for Greg to let Jennifer know his feelings.

What followed is recounted below. At the time of these interviews, shortly after their marriage, Greg and Jennifer were living nearby, still working at the Monastery, and considering what it meant to no longer be monks.

Jennifer: I had been practicing as a monk for over five years, and about four months ago, I received a letter from Greg asking me to marry him. Apparently, he had been considering it for quite a while, but I didn't know that. Even though marriage or a relationship with Greg was not something I had consciously considered before, I knew the answer was yes; there wasn't any hesitation. There was a lot of upheaval and emotion, but in and of itself, the act of saying yes was clear and simple.

I have had similar experiences before when I've made decisions that haven't felt like decisions. Coming to the Monastery is an example. It didn't feel like anything big or wrenching, it just felt like the next thing to do. Each time I've moved to a new place or changed jobs, the ones that have worked out the best were those that felt most right in my heart, when I could be still enough to listen.

An important aspect of this decision was not believing the conditioning that says there's a right way to proceed with someone before you decide to get married, that you're supposed to get to know each other in a certain way, which is generally quite different from spending five years together in silence. My brother said, "How did you get to know each other without talking?" Well, you ought to try it some time—I'd recommend it to anyone! Greg and I know each other pretty well, in a very unusual way. Being here doing monastic training with others has always felt so intimate to me. That is what made the "yes" possible.

Someone said to me after we were married, "You look really happy—it must be because you're married." It seems to me that I was able to get married because the happiness was there first. Otherwise, I would not have been able to say yes to this opportunity; I wouldn't have had the confidence to answer from my heart. My being able to is due to this spiritual practice.

The first time I talked with Cheri about getting married, she grilled me (compassionately) with all kinds of questions, as she is known to do sometimes in guidance. It felt like a test. Finally, the only thing I could say was that getting married seemed like the next step on my path. In one way, it was a huge change, and in another it was simply adding something to what I was already doing.

Although I wanted this relationship to be within the context of spiritual practice, I told Cheri I had no idea what that meant or how it would work. She said we'd have to see. The "we" was comforting, suggesting that it could happen within our practice and possibilities for that could be explored. So that's what we have been doing—watching it unfold, not knowing what form it will take.

In addition to the transition from living by myself for five years to living closely with someone, there's the huge change of not living at the Monastery. We still work here, but most importantly, we still have the practice. We acknowledged that formally when Cheri did a wedding ceremony for us and we accepted the Buddhist precepts as vows to guide us in our marriage.

It would be a false conclusion to say that everybody should have a partner. Where does that idea come from? If relationship is the opportunity at hand, we can practice with that. If not, we can still practice. Those are simply different life situations; neither is right or wrong, better or worse.

Last night I had a seizure of self-hate, stemming from a belief that I hadn't done enough or should have done something better, it was all up to me, I should have taken control, and I failed. Now and then I could step back and breathe and watch myself be stuck in that process. Greg just sat there listening. Occasionally he would say or ask something, but basically he was just there. No matter what he said or did at that point, no matter how loving it was, I would not have seen it until I was willing to find acceptance within myself. In fact, I may have taken anything he said as just the opposite of loving, because that was what was going on within me. If I'm not in touch with love in myself, I won't be able to take it in from someone else.

Cheri has been encouraging me to keep paying attention to what I want. That's something I hadn't done much of for five years, because I didn't think monks were supposed to want. My sense of what she's saying is, now that you've chosen this as something you want to do, keeping looking to follow your heart. Living as a monk, I was trying so hard to live up to my idea of being open and good and wise and perfect that I was restricting myself. I can see I've done a lot of things in my life that same way: thinking I'd found the answer to freedom but restricting myself by trying so hard to do it right. Being in a close relationship helps me be aware of this, by giving me a new context for considering what I truly want.

Greg: People have asked, how could it happen that in silence you develop a relationship with somebody and decide to get married? Well, it's not like it was the first thing that popped into my head or that I became unhappy and said, "I think I'll quit this business, get married, and do something else." It was more the process of paying attention to something that kept coming into my awareness. I spent over a year working with this, trying to make it go away, because I held this idea that being a monk was the best way to live, and it was wrong to fall in love, and pursuing that would be taking a step backward. But, eventually, taking that step, and being willing to live with the consequences, was the only way I could move ahead.

In moving toward realizing my aspiration of being married to Jennifer, I thought I was going to fail, that it wouldn't work, she would say no, somehow it wouldn't happen. I was so focused on, "Am I going to ask her, or am I not?" To ask her required a big leap of faith, all the faith I could muster. What it came down to in the end was that if I decided not to pursue it, it would be turning away from a part of myself. I was prepared to go through being crushed if her answer was no, and I was also very much wanting and expecting to hear back yes.

When I sent Jennifer the letter, I didn't think of how it would affect the other people here. Any group of people develops its own system of relating to each other, and that system has been stirred up by our getting married. At first I was surprised and upset that it had such a disturbing effect. Now I see that it was bound to be disturbing, which is not necessarily bad.

On the other hand, it is wonderful to do this practice with another person. I'm finding out that's possible, although sometimes with Jennifer it's a little more—ah, brutal, I might say. I'll be rambling on and on, completely caught in conditioning, and Jennifer (she denies this) says something like, "You know, it's getting pretty boring hearing you say the same thing over and over again."

Being in a relationship is also helpful in showing me certain conditioned ways of acting. Often, if I'm paying attention, I kind of know what's going to happen next, and I have a choice of saying harmful words or not, writing a mean note or not, offering to help or not, following my conditioning or not. With Jennifer, the same conditioning arises, but it's so clear that I don't want to be mean to her, I do want to be helpful to her, and it's easier to not continue with my conditioned patterns. Then I say, how about trying this with Phyl and Cameron and Tom and other people? I may have chosen to say harmful words by telling myself, well, so-and-so is just surly, so I don't need to be kind in return. In fact, there are times when Jennifer seems surly, too, but I don't abuse her. Noticing this helps me realize that I don't want to do things that are hurtful, to anybody.

Something we learn in this practice is that when we don't know what to do, it's probably good not to do anything. But sometimes you can't know what the next step is until you act first, which was true in this case. It was good for me to go against that idea of doing nothing as the more spiritual approach. Doing nothing would have been a way to hide; it seemed safer because I was afraid that in pursuing this I would lose everything, in a sense. I had a lot invested in being a monk, being a hot Zen student, stuff like that, and I was afraid that if I entered into a relationship I would lose all that.

And, in fact, I did. That's where a lot of my practice is now: my role at the Monastery has completely changed. Aside from not having the identity of a monk any longer, I'm not in charge of anything now. I sort of don't know who I am anymore. That's happening a lot lately, and I think for me it's good. Not that it's some sort of end, but it's in contrast to having built up this structure in which I was very certain of what was going on and who I was.

Right now everything feels more intense, I'm more sensitive, almost raw, as if I have no skin. So it's a great opportunity to work on my attachment to a particular identity. I hope it will be a little more difficult to simply step into the next comfortable identity that comes along.

Almost everybody thinks that if only they were monks, they would be doing better at spiritual practice. It's true that being in a monastery setting can be helpful, but being a monk certainly doesn't guarantee anything. Some people won't try being a monk because they feel they don't deserve to have the experience of being clear and centered, that it's not possible for them because of some way they are. Other people decide that being a monk is the right way to do it, so they go through the motions, meditate a lot, look at things in a certain way, and assume they've done it. But as long as there is an assumption that being a monk is something special, something that not everybody can do, or I'm pretty good because I'm doing this, or I have to be a monk because I'm worse than everybody—anything like that is a hindrance to seeing how things are.

Cheri talks a lot about how it doesn't really matter what you do, as long as you're paying attention to it. I guess I didn't really believe that, because I thought it was better to be in a monastery than to be somewhere else. In my last few guidance sessions with Cheri, I asked her, "Well, what do you want me to do now?" And she always says, "I just want you to do spiritual practice."

One of the least expected effects of living as a monk, perhaps, is that one's capacity for life is not narrowed but expanded. Over time, sharp edges and rough surfaces of egocentric defense systems are worn and smoothed, the wall protecting identity falls away, the membrane defining self softens and dissolves. One develops the ability to be ever more fully present simultaneously to oneself and to others. Monastic life, quite unexpectedly, serves human relationships because it makes possible degrees of sensitivity, respect, and kindness, along with capacities for both interdependence and individual growth that seem impossible anywhere else.

◇

Cameron

In 1989, Cameron took leave from her job to spend six months pursuing intensive spiritual practice at the Zen Center's rural retreat facility. Only after arriving did she learn that silence is observed all the time, not just during retreats, and that what had been called simply "the land" was being referred to as "the Monastery." Cameron stayed on, became a monk, and remained one for seven years. Faced with many unexpected developments, including major illness, she came to recognize how the same conditioned patterns of belief determined her responses to all her experience.

1992

Before I came here, I had this idea that I needed to know how to do something before I could do it. Of course, that makes it hard to do anything new, and it didn't work here, because there's just too much to be done. For me, this place offers a whole new approach: looking at something and trying to see what needs to be accomplished, what kind of tools might work for the task, just figuring it out—and I absolutely love it. It's so freeing that there's not a right way to do things, that you can figure it out as you go along. I'm still working with the fear of "doing it wrong," however; that seems to be a life-long challenge.

When I hadn't been here long, I got the job of cleaning out the water tank. You have to climb up on this tower where there's just a little wooden edge around the tank, then you climb a ladder to the top of the tank and lower a footstool down into it through a small hole. Then you lower yourself down onto the footstool inside the tank. I am intensely claustrophobic, and when I said I'd do this job, I thought the whole top of the tank came off. I cannot describe the terror that gripped me when I climbed up there and saw that little hole. I knew that if I had to go down in there, I would die. So I got

down, my heart pounding, and I went to Greg, who was work director at the time, and said I simply could not do it.

I expected Greg to say, "Oh, okay, we'll get somebody else to do it." But he looked at me and said, "I don't know what to say." I walked away thinking, "What does that mean?" I figured it meant I had to do it. So I did it. And I didn't die.

I'm still claustrophobic, and when I am in that kind of situation, I feel fear. But the fact that I did it and got through it (and it wasn't even that bad once I got in there) makes it easier for me to do other things I am afraid to do. I never would have gone through with it in any other situation, and I think a crucial part of that was being left to have my own experience. Nobody said, "Too bad, you have to do it anyway." Greg just didn't buy into the idea of my inadequacy.

I think that attitude helped me allow myself to have the fear, and allow myself to do the job in a way that was considerate toward that scared person I was in that moment. I dropped the stool down into the tank, and then went slowly, one step at a time, and gradually acclimated myself to being in that space. Every once in a while I would climb up the footstool and poke my head out the top and take some breaths when I started to feel that I couldn't breathe and might die. I could have freaked out if I'd forced myself, pushed myself too hard, which I had done in other situations. But somehow I approached it with compassion, and it worked.

Every time I do something new and find whatever amount of success I find in it, it makes me more confident in myself and my ability to be in any situation and do whatever needs to be done. Previously, I was often amazed at how much people did in life, because I thought somehow or other they'd gotten trained for all these things. I wouldn't have had the nerve to just go and do something without knowing how; I thought that somebody had to show me and I had to practice and get good at it first.

It's been the same with spiritual practice. I started coming here for retreats, thinking that maybe some day, way off in the future, I could come and practice full time, after I'd learned all these things that would make me successful at meditation. When Cheri told me that doing this spiritual practice full time was a possibility right then and there, I was astonished. That was almost three years ago.

◇

Several months ago, Cheri told me that two of the monks who had been at the Monastery from its beginning were getting married— to each other. This, for me, was one of the first of those experiences in spiritual practice where the entire house of cards constructed by ego comes tumbling down in one fell swoop. I was incredulous. I remember feeling that Cheri might as well have told me to turn around and look at a giraffe standing in the meadow behind me as to say that these two monks were to be married. Neither of the two statements would have made any more or less sense than the other.

A righteous voice in my head was saying things like, "This is a *spiritual* community. We don't even talk to one another. How could two of us decide to form an intimate partnership? Relationships don't happen in a monastery." A lot of things I felt strongly about in terms of maintaining a spiritual community were just swept away by this. Another voice took me back to being really, really little and feeling abandoned and unloved. I felt wronged; love was happening somewhere else, and I was left out of it.

I was so inspired by Phyllis's response to the situation. She and the two people who got married had personal connections going way back; the three of them were the first monks here. I watched her dig into her practice through this whole thing, and the strength that came out was truly awe-inspiring. It's shown me that this practice works.

The biggest challenge for me was a lot of personal feelings that came up about relationships. My relationships were a series of hopes followed by disappointments: hopes that I would find happiness because of the relationship, and disappointment because I never did. I came to this practice looking to find a way to be happy with myself. In fact, this is the only environment I've ever been in where it doesn't seem to matter whether you were a man or a woman, heterosexual or homosexual; it is a completely leveling environment, with everybody doing the same thing and doing it individually. It seemed to be an environment where "relationships," at least as I had known them, didn't even exist.

My relationship issues seemed to have faded into the background, but with this announcement about two monks planning to be married, they blossomed forth in full body. Here I am entering menopause as a celibate person—is this what I really want? If I keep going on this path will I ever have a relationship? Does that matter? It seemed very much as if it did matter all of a sudden when two people were going off in the evening to be together, and I was all alone in my little hermitage.

After the marriage, there were just two of us left living at the Monastery. At first I was not sure whether Cheri would want to keep offering us the opportunity to stay here. We don't have many people coming to utilize the Monastery, and I think Cheri is feeling that if this isn't a place where people want to be, it doesn't make sense having it. She has talked about keeping it open for a year once the building is finished, to see if that makes a difference. With a dormitory and dining room, it will be more convenient and protected from the extremes of weather, and there will be bathrooms, so you won't have to pee in a bucket.

◇

There was a turning point for me at the New Year's retreat at Carmel. Each night, everybody sat facing the inside of the room instead of facing the wall, with a different person in the guide's seat each time. We went around the room with each of the fifteen or so people asking the spiritual question that was up for them at that point, and the person in the guide's seat responded. Being in the guide's seat was not something I had any desire to do; I did not volunteer, I was told I was to do it. For my ego, the experience was devastating. The image that comes to mind is being made of glass and being hit with a hammer and shattering into a million slivers. What I saw was that the entire time I've been training, ego has been in charge. I've been trying to do this practice right, just as I'd tried to do everything else in life, so people would like and respect me. I'm not sure why I saw that so clearly then; maybe it was that my responses to the questions didn't feel as if they were coming from something authentic in me.

This is a painful true confession: I wanted Cheri to look at me and know, "Here's one person who's able to do this kind of work and be helpful." Cheri has so much responsibility and so much work and so many people to help, and my feeling was that I wanted to do well to prove that I could be helpful to her. Instead, it was this humiliating experience of being just the opposite of that, feeling I was one more person she has to drag along for a few more years. I felt that my ego was exposed, raw and puny, to all those people. Sitting in the front of the room that night I felt like the Wizard of Oz: there's this booming voice and puffs of smoke, and everybody's trembling with awe of this powerful being, then the curtain pulls back, and it's this puny little man who's pulling levers. I started to see how my whole life process is directed externally, how I always look outward for approval, and how inside—the authentic part of me—is not attended to at all.

I continued to feel shattered for almost two weeks after that. Every time I would try to do something, I was aware that it was ego doing it. Ego had been wiped out, but then, slowly and subtly, I watched it regroup.

I had been work director for almost two years, and it is the responsibility of the work director, via written notes, to assign all the daily work to the monks, residents, and guests. There seems to be such a great deal of work—prepare meals, teach classes, grow a garden, build a rammed-earth building, maintain the tractor, tools, and solar equipment—and it can seem both important and impossible to get it all done. Ego saw all that responsibility as something it could get righteous about, something to grasp onto to feel important again. Once I felt that I was doing things "right" again, I lost that sense of devastation.

Then Cheri suggested that it would be good training for all of us to rotate the work director job, to give everybody a chance to experience it. The first day, I received a job assignment from the new work director, I took my note, did my job, paid attention to what I was doing, and enjoyed my work experience. In doing so, I realized that is how I could have been doing the job of work director all along. Instead, I had become involved in noticing how others were working, feeling that the results of everyone else's work somehow reflected how well I was doing my job as work director.

Cheri has told me a zillion times that my job is to stay centered. She's told us all that the work is for our training, and it doesn't matter what gets done and what doesn't. In the heat of things, when the concrete truck is on the way and more people are needed than are available, I would lose sight of that completely. But in that one day, I saw how taking it all so seriously wasn't necessary.

All my life I've had this sense of being a hypocrite, not being sincere, and it's because there's the other whole part of me that's completely denied—the part that isn't the good spiritual student or the person who gets things done and does everything right. I don't suspect that my "shadow" side is any worse than the shadow stuff everybody has—greed, hatred, and delusion, in Buddhist terms— but for this person that I've been conditioned to be, it's so difficult to look at. My work right now is to claim that part of me and accept it. I have no idea in the world how to even get near it, it's so completely unacceptable. So it's a challenging little project. But now I'm kind of excited, experiencing the possibility of loving and accepting *all* of this being, and how different life might be.

1996

I was diagnosed with breast cancer a year and a half ago. I haven't talked much to anybody about what it's like to go through a serious illness and be living at the Monastery, since this spiritual practice involves silence.

Living here in this healthy lifestyle, with pure food and physical activity and meditation, to discover cancer growing in me—talk about finding out there's no control! Immediately I wanted to make it something outside my spiritual practice: cancer is a *real* problem, it's time to stop all this spiritual stuff and deal with this.

Cheri, as she's famous for doing, stayed the line. At first I was shocked and horrified. But eventually I realized that fear had pulled me right back into my conditioned reactions, and the way I wanted to deal with this was the way I'd always dealt with everything. Cheri saw ego at work there and refused to go along with it. And of course now I'm very grateful.

The same duality had been operating in me all along: between wanting to do a spiritual practice, wanting to be free, wanting to be a person who is able to live in the moment, and, on the other hand, wanting to be comfortable, wanting life not to be hard, feeling that I'm too old for this, it's time to let up on myself and take it easy. It's not surprising that the cancer diagnosis amplified that conflict. I'd imagined that all you need to drop your petty ego concerns and have your life turned around is to hear that you have a life-threatening illness; you read about that kind of thing. But what's happened with me is that both sides of the duality have become more insistent. If I have only a couple of years to live, do I want to be here sweating and working, or do I want to be comfortable somewhere else? Ego says, we don't have long to live; we have to take care of ourselves. And the other side says, we don't have long to live; we'd better get free.

After the diagnosis, I was out in the world for most of the next year. First, I had to deal with things like not having any money or insurance. Then, after the surgery, I needed to be somewhere clean to protect the wounds during my recuperation, so I stayed with a couple who live nearby and often spend time at the Monastery. Because the cancer had already metastasized to my lymph system, I was on chemotherapy for six months, then I was in the Bay Area for seven weeks of radiation treatment.

While my body was undergoing all this change, everything also changed here at the Monastery. When I left, the kitchen was still in the tent, and Phyl and I were the only monks. When I came back, this place was totally transformed: everything has been moved from the tent into the new building, and a lot of people have come to train, and Phyl is a completely different person.

I don't know whether it was the effects of chemotherapy or the difficulty of the spiritual challenge—probably both—but my mind was fuzz when I came back here. All of the routines are different now, and I didn't know how to do anything. I felt completely lost, as if whoever I was—all the things that told me who I was, that made me feel okay in the world, that made me feel I belonged to this place in terms of contributing to its organization—all that was gone.

In little ways and big ways, I've just had to let go, let go, let go. With the lymph nodes removed, my arm is compromised in terms of its immune response, and I was warned about getting any cuts or scrapes or even a pulled cuticle. I imagined I would be assigned to things like typing schedules, but the first assignment I got was to make all the trim for the windows and doors for the inside and outside of the whole building. I was feeling as if I hardly knew my name, and I was going to be working with power tools? I was terrified about something happening to my arm. But my role as a monk now is to accept what I'm told, bow, no coming up with better ideas about how things should be done. So off I went. And now I'm working in the shop quite comfortably.

I'm just beginning to get little tastes of freedom. I've had my face pushed into everything ego believes it cannot stand. An example occurred this morning in meditation. Chemotherapy puts you directly into menopause, and added to the heat of the summer here, hot flashes are intense. My body heats up, my heart races, and I break out into a full sweat. Today sweat was soaking my hair and my clothes, and there was the feeling of, "I can't stand this." I want to get up, get a drink, take my clothes off, douse myself in water, anything to make me feel better. But I can't; I'm sitting in meditation. It feels like more than a person ought to have to endure. On top of that, a mosquito comes. It's whining around my head and lands on my cheek.

Then there was the realization that this is what I do in my whole life: I set up a line, I stretch myself to it, and I say this is as far as I can go. But there's always something more—there's always that mosquito. At that point, I bail out on myself. What the practice is bringing me to realize is that there can be no line. Acceptance and compassion have to be there regardless.

It's hard only because ego resists. After meditation, I went into the dining room and got some granola with a fresh peach on it and sat out on the back porch, enjoying life, right after the experience of "I can't stand this" in the meditation hall. So, that sense that I can't stand it simply isn't true; it is a product of the conditioned mind.

I just had a wonderful experience when I was given the assignment to make the attic vents for the building. There are six of them, and they are odd-shaped, with slats that come in at angles. It was completely beyond anything I thought I could do; I couldn't figure out how to approach it, even what tools to use. The vent job became my whole practice. I would think, "I don't know how to do this." I'd try one thing, and that didn't work, so I'd try something else. I had to make a jig, a thing to cut the slats in—I even had to make the tool to use! I kept trying, and eventually I got them all done, then realized that I had made half of them backwards. So, I had to make another jig, with a different angle, and take more lumber and make more slats. Somebody in me wanted to run out of here, to say, "This is too hard!" But I would just say to that part of myself that was so upset, "It's okay. Let's just see what's possible. How about trying this? Well, that didn't work. What about this? That doesn't work either. How about this?" Eventually I got it done. And I am so tickled with those things. I just stayed with that person in me who was afraid to be in the shop, who felt she didn't know how to do anything any more; I went through it with her step by step to the completion, which was really good training. I feel that something is different in me for having gone through that process.

As weak as I felt when I came back here, as hard as it's been, as much as I wanted to give up at times, I didn't.

When I look at Phyl, I see what is possible, and that has been like a life raft for me. I've seen Phyl do it—I've seen her go through this training and come out on the other side. Of course Cheri has done it, but I didn't see Cheri's process, so for all I know, she was born that way. But Phyl I watched. When I first came here, I projected that a lot of things were hard for Phyl. I saw her be just as ego-identified as anybody and go through a grueling process of letting go. Now she seems to breeze through things that used to present obstacles, and I experience a sense of calm and confidence from her that I never experienced before.

The *sangha* [spiritual community] has been absolutely wonderful. There has been so much connection and love in this whole process that I feel that I'm exactly where I need to be. And I'm starting to feel the freedom in not needing all those things I thought I needed. When I got back here and it seemed that everything was gone, of course that was only ego's perspective. What really happened is that now I can have the kind of training where I just focus on what's going on with me. I don't have to think about whether we need propane today and who's arriving tomorrow and when we can repair a hermitage. My ego ran me ragged with all that trying to be good, trying to earn my acceptance, a lot of it without my conscious awareness. Now I have this opportunity just to train. And finally I am able to see it as a gift.

Building as Dharma

For most of the time that the Monastery has been in existence, a great deal of the monks' work, spiritual and physical, has involved building. First the individual hermitages and then the central building complex served as arenas for ongoing mindfulness practice. In the new complex, the meditation hall links taller buildings that house the kitchen and dining hall at one end and the dormitory at the other. The completion of "the building," as it is called, marked the end of the period in which group functions took place in large tents.

The building grew out of the land. The massive walls are made of earth dug from the site to make room for the foundation. Their rough-textured grays, tans, ochres, and siennas, like the redwood of the window and door frames and the clay tiles of the floors and roof, evoke the natural continuum in which we exist. Cloister walkways meander around the perimeter, a permeable edge linking the interior spaces to the world beyond.

Dharma means "law" in the sense of natural law, or the way things are; it is commonly used to refer to the teachings of the Buddha. In many ways, the building is a reflection of the dharma. Its existence is based in persistent attentiveness and individual effort. The proportions express generosity. Beams are joined with admirable straightforwardness. There is an ease in how things function; doors open and close smoothly and silently.

From the beginning, Cheri made it clear to the monks that the building itself—the process, not the product—was their practice. The following group interview took place in the early stages of construction, when the walls were being rammed.

Greg: I'm supposed to be in charge of getting this building done. At first, I was going crazy, because I had a certain schedule in my head, and a lot of expectations, and people clearly didn't know what they were doing, including me. It was awful. It's been eleven months since we started, and finally I'm beginning to see how holding an idea about how quickly everything ought to happen contributed greatly to my suffering. And I'm sure to others'.

At one point, when I was really upset about trying to keep to my schedule, Cheri said she would rather that the building never get built than construct a monument to my egocentricity.

Phyllis: And she meant it!

Greg: Part of my practice now is to find compassion within the role of being in charge. If someone gets injured, or someone gets upset because I yelled at them, if I am paying attention, I'll be able to respond in a compassionate way. And when I can find compassion toward someone else, I can find it for myself; it helps me see how uncaring it is to put that kind of pressure on anyone, myself or others.

Some of what we do is dangerous, which can be helpful in learning to keep our attention in the present moment. Standing up high on the building or using heavy tools or machinery, you may feel fear, and here you are encouraged to deal with that in a different way. Men, for example, often believe that if you show fear, somebody might put you down, so you just brute through it or ignore it or avoid circumstances where you would be afraid. Here, when fear comes up, we pay attention to it, try to see what it's all about.

The interesting thing is, when we are mindful of it in that way, it sort of disappears—not that you become dumb and careless, but ideas about who you are because of the fear no longer get in your way.

To get the concrete poured for the bond beam, somebody had to be up on top of the building, where wires and boards made it difficult to walk. I don't like heights and I'm not all that agile, and it scared me. But I found that it's identifying with the fear that's dangerous; worrying about what could happen, for example, could get me into trouble, make me trip or lose my balance. So, when I was up there pouring the concrete, I was practicing as hard as I could to stay centered in the present moment.

Being afraid that I'm going to fall doesn't mean that I am going to fall; feeling fear doesn't have to stop me from going up there and doing things that seem scary. This building is a great teacher for all of us in that way. We spend so much time trying to protect ourselves from risk, from sickness, from death, trying to arrange life so nothing can happen to us. But that is like putting ourselves in a cage that separates us from life.

Phyllis: If I allow my attention to cling to a sensation, whether it's fear or whatever, a chain reaction is set into motion, from sensation to thought to emotion to action, and then I become completely identified that "I" who is afraid. But if I bring my attention back and watch all that, I can see that only part of me is having the experience of being afraid. By maintaining mindfulness, all of the parts of me can be embraced, and I don't need to identify with the fear.

Jennifer: I often drive the tractor, and moving this large vehicle, raising this huge bucket toward where people are standing, is real incentive to stay mindful. If I'm not present, the chance of an accident is much greater. I had a great deal of fear at first. When Cheri asked me if I was ready to drive the tractor, I said no. Within a few weeks, the tractor manual was in my mail slot with directions to read it. I understood that this was going to be my job, whether I was ready or not. Then the process of being with the fear began. Fear comes up all the time when I'm on the tractor. But now the fear doesn't replace mindfulness; it's more just a sensation that goes along with doing that kind of work. Mindfulness actually seems heightened because the fear is there.

Greg: Another way the building teaches me is that there isn't such a thing as being finished, like you wake up one day and the work is over and nothing happens any more. For a long time, that was my idea of spiritual practice, that I would get enlightened, end my suffering, then it would all be finished.

It's also true that it *is* possible to do that *in each moment:* wake up, end suffering right now—and right now, and right now. It's the same with the building: right now we need the pile of dirt here, we put it here, we're finished, we don't worry about how we did it or what will happen tomorrow or what the schedule says, we go on to whatever is the next thing. Right now, we can be completely present, and there is no problem. That approach makes it easy to see how so much of suffering is created in our minds.

◇

From inside the building, the land touches human senses through casement windows that open toward distant hills, or into pine and live oaks and manzanita, or onto the courtyard, where a doe and her fawns come each morning to graze. From the outside, the building cannot be seen in its entirety from any point. It is experienced as a succession of images, impressions, sensations. Dark wood against white walls. The whisper of soft shoes on tile. Stepping through shadows striping a sunlit porch; turning a corner into the elegant space of an arched entryway. The firm weight of a door handle, and the flicker of reflections in glass panes as the door swings open. A ripple of tiled roof silhouetted against the night sky.

A high, beamed ceiling embraces the disparate contents of the dining hall in a handsome harmony: worn wooden tables and benches from the old kitchen tent join company with an antique cabinet, an elaborately carved oak table where food is served, and the handmade plates, bowls, and mugs. The kitchen too has a high ceiling, in consideration, perhaps, of those who cooked and washed dishes for years under the heavy dark slope of canvas tent. Now there is a spacious, solid, and safe shelter for the fundamental work of preparing food.

People remark on not only the beauty of the building but also its emanations of peace and clarity and compassion. In a discussion recorded in the new meditation hall when the building was near completion, Cheri and two of the monks described how those qualities were embedded in the very process of construction.

Cameron: When I came here, Phyl was assigned to make the plans for a new hermitage and get it built. I was assigned to help her. We got the piers lined up and the frame up and the door in, then Cheri came down to look at it.

Right after that, we had guidance appointments, and I went in for guidance first. Cheri said that the door to the hermitage was in the wrong place and had to be moved. I thought, "We've already built it—how can we move the door? It's already there." I left guidance a wreck, and I was sure this was going to upset Phyl; it was her design and she was in charge of the whole project.

I went back to the hermitage and waited for Phyl, because we were going to continue working. I was watching for her to come down the path, expecting her to look dejected, maybe angry. But when she came, she was smiling. I thought Cheri must have forgotten to give her the bad news, but Phyl said, in this matter of fact way, "We have to move the door." I was so surprised, but I could see that to her, it was no big deal. That was a very helpful lesson for me.

Cheri: First of all, learning that you *could* move a door. And second, that you could do it cheerfully.

Cameron: And it really wasn't hard. The door just had to go from here to there, and we set about doing it. Phyl's response—or lack of it—had quite an impact on me.

Cheri: An incident like that leaves you puzzled, questioning. How does this work? How could a person be this way? How does a person get to that state of acceptance?

Phyllis: There are two extremes in how we respond to a job like that. One is giving up too soon, thinking, "It's too hard, it's just going to have to be this way, I can't do any better." The other is having my ego so involved that the work has to be perfect, I'm not willing to accept anything less, which goes way beyond what is necessary. But the internal process is the same, whether we're driving ourselves to make it perfect or down on ourselves because we feel incapable of doing it right. The practice is to find the middle way, where we do it for the love of doing it; we do it not because of our ideas about it, but for the building itself.

Cheri: And that's the way we can live each moment of our lives.

Phyllis: On this building, if you look closely, you'll see that some of the rafters are cut a little differently, and that's fine. At one time, people who had never hammered a nail were working here, and to create frustration for them is not what this is all about. There's a way in which my practice can be aligned with whatever ability is available, a point of harmony and balance between perfection and possibility.

Cheri: When one is completely in the moment, it *is* perfection. And the result is irrelevant.

Phyllis: When you're doing it that way, you're kind of in love—in love with every wall, every board, every nail.

Cheri: We could have had a fundraising campaign and hired professionals and gone into debt, and the building would have been finished sooner, and we would walk in, and what would we have? It would be like getting someone else to live your life for you.

It is impossible to look at this building, to be around it and inside it, and not sense something about this practice. That has been achieved, I think, by staying with the practice every step of the way. In a spontaneous little dharma talk today with some of the monks, I was saying that there is never a letter that goes out, not a flyer, not a quick note dashed off that does not reflect the practice. If the time comes for a letter to be mailed, say, and it's not as it needs to be, the response is not, "Oh, well, I'll do better next time." That letter doesn't go out yet. The same with the building: if it's not as it should be, well, we just keep doing it until it is.

It's the *doing* that's so terribly interesting anyway, not having it done. It's the attitude of mind with which we do it, our attention, our care, the loving-kindness that goes into it—all that is a reflection of what motivates us, of where we are now in our practice as well as where we want to be. When someone sees what has been built, when they are in its presence, they will sense all that has gone into bringing it into being. Therefore, there is nothing that does not matter, there is nothing that is not critical. Our honor and respect for the practice enables us to be present to the work in a way that will allow that loving-kindness to come through us, through what we produce, to others.

◇

Mary

Mary began attending meditation retreats in North Carolina in the mid-1980s and took Buddhist precepts at the Monastery in 1990. Her fifteen years in a landscaping business gave her experience in project coordination, and in 1994, Cheri suggested that Mary continue her spiritual practice at the Monastery where she would be in charge of bringing the building to completion. Mary has been there ever since.

1996

Recently I've recognized my need to be a hero, especially in the context of being in charge of the building project. I came out here with a small amount of knowledge and a large amount of willingness (the monk in me is very proud of my willingness) and the intention to finish the building. At the same time, I'm humble: I'm going to "help" finish the building, "facilitate" the finishing of the building. That was supposed to happen in six months, and after two years, the building still isn't finished, which is truly humbling.

Now that all the decisions are made and what's left to do is just go on driving in nails, there's nothing challenging in it for me. And, interestingly enough, I can't stand this place right now: I want out, I want this project to be over, I'm sick of this.

In the rest of my life, I do the same thing. Whether it's a letter that takes an hour or a landscape project that takes a year, I accept a task and approach it heroically. I'm the one who can do the thing that is so hard to do. But once it gets beyond the heroic, it no longer supports that identity for me, so I don't want to do it any more. I want to go off and do other heroic things. I also have the belief that I have to finish anything I start. So, again and again, I get in the double bind of hating a project but having to do it.

I hadn't realized until a few days ago how that hero scenario is played out in everything I undertake. I keep thinking, "Once the building passes inspection, then I can finally just be a monk." But probably I'll take on the identity of a heroic monk, and then I'll have to deal with that [laughing].

There's a whole set of beliefs about what monks are, how I should be as a monk, how I'm perceived if I'm a monk, what being a monk means, that I'm more spiritual as a monk than I am out in the world, that I have a very important job as a monk, which is to awaken. I want to appear a certain way to fit in with what I project to be other people's idea of a monk.

But my identity as a monk not only serves ego, it also serves the process of awakening, in that it requires me to be as present and aware as I can possibly be. So, good deal: I can allow that identity to be there, and because it's the identity of a monk, in itself it involves dissolving the identity.

All the attributes I assume are part of the identity of a monk come to my attention, because, in fact, I am not those things. My practice as a monk is to be as present as I can to that situation, with compassion. I can't just say, "Monks are supposed to be serene. I am not serene. Therefore I am A) not a monk, or B) a bad monk." Maybe the answer is C): my belief about what monks are is incorrect. I have to look at all the reactions and assumptions and attachments associated with that identity. Whereas my identity as a landscaper doesn't require me to consider any of that.

So, at the moment, a voice from ego is saying, "I want to get out of here." But if I'm going to repeat this process—the hero scenario and the suffering it involves—I might as well repeat it here, where there is so much encouragement to look it in the face and get free from it.

What Cheri does best is point out to me when I'm indulging in egocentricity, giving in to my conditioning, which is to hate the whole project at this point but beat myself until it is finished. And *never* allow myself to feel good about my work. Sometimes I can allow myself to experience those feelings, to accept everything that is happening in me when I lack confidence, am frightened, don't feel heroic. At those times, meditation—just sitting on the cushion—is such a relief. I can just sit there and not have to figure anything out.

1998

I've been noticing what happens in the process of being pulled away from awareness. I bring my attention to the present moment, and I don't like something that's going on—the sensation of pain in my back, say. I have thoughts about it, like wanting something to be different as a way to relieve that pain, and I have emotions in response to the thoughts, like fear. Acting on that emotion turns me away from the awareness; if I'm afraid of what's going to happen, the tendency is to leave that experience and go to something else, like worry. It's hard to have the bare sensation without the belief that it *is* pain, it *is* bad, it *does* mean something about how long I can continue to sit here, I may be crippled for life, I'm going to die. That's the progression: there's a little pain in my chest, thirty seconds later I'm having a heart attack, I haven't made out a will, I'm in serious trouble. Those kinds of beliefs are what pull us away from the present moment.

Staying with the sensation, thought, and emotion is almost like standing in an electrical field, to borrow a term from Susan. It feels very intense, very loud, there's *so much* sensation that it's frightening to some part of me. The habitual way to get out of the discomfort and fear is to attach meaning to it, like, "I may be losing my mind," and then, *ploonk*—I'm pulled right out of the present again. What is not usually recognized is how much suffering and misery there is anywhere *but* the present moment.

If I'm willing to stay with the bombardment of sensation, thought, and emotion, inside all that, at the center, it's incredibly quiet. That depth of silence becomes my refuge, rather than something I'm frightened of. How that happens I have not a clue, but it has something to do with the willingness not to believe in the fear, to stay present with the sensation, or to come back diligently to it.

"Silence" might not describe everybody's experience of what it's like at the center, but that's the word that comes to me. It's like being in a big crowd of people—an arena or athletic stadium or a shopping center—where so much is going on and it's so intense, then within that, there's a moment when it's completely still, because I'm present to all of it but I'm not drawn out to any of it. There's a sense of nothing lacking, no problem, no difficulty, no bottom to it, no end to it, no conditions placed on it; nothing is out of place, even raging emotions, violence, depression, tenderness, all of it is there—there's no limit on life. I suspect that we have all experienced something like this in some form or another, if only just a glimpse. I think it is the universal human spiritual experience.

An awareness practice involves moving to that experience of silence intentionally, rather than running into it randomly. If that's something we want to experience in a deliberate, conscious way, there are certain things that facilitate that, and one is being in a monastic environment, where there is a lot of external silence. I've wondered if the silence of the Monastery reflects that deep internal silence

I know exactly where I want to go: through that intense field of sensation-thought-emotion to the heart of the silence. And I know what pulls me away from it: the beliefs and reactions of my conditioning. Along with the physical sensations come my conditioned beliefs about what they mean and what will happen to me if I stay present to my experience. So I want to maintain awareness of those beliefs as well.

◇

A great thing about working here is that as soon as you figure out what your job description is, the whole structure shifts so you can't get too attached to it. I've been trying for a long time to pin down exactly what it is that I'm supposed to be doing. We all want to know what is expected of us so we can get it right and be okay. I want to know, am I responsible for this, or is someone else responsible? But here nobody gives me that answer, because what I really want to know is what I'm *not* responsible for, so I don't have to pay attention to that part of my experience. Monastic training is designed to encourage paying attention to all of it.

Because the role of work director involves assigning people tasks and generally overseeing how things are done, people think of it as a big job. But is it really a big job, or does my ego make it a big job? I've noticed that ego can take the fact that a lot is going on and actually create difficulty, turning "a lot going on" into "a big, difficult job." It tells me, "You're a person who has a big, hard, important job. If you were to walk out the door tomorrow, they'd really miss you." I've become a somebody, a special person, separate and defined. I can almost feel the sheer bulk of my identity!

It's true that there are a lot of things to get done, a lot to be attentive to, and yet it doesn't have to be hard. I'm aware that when I'm not feeling needed or not getting enough attention, I'll make my job hard to create a sense of self-importance. That can be a clue to me that I need to give myself more attention—not in a selfish, self-centered way, but just that I need to attend to what's going on with this person.

I thought once the building was finished, my relationship to my job might be different, but it isn't. I remain very project-oriented, I love to be intensely focused, I love to work hard on something, and then when it's over—move on! So it was interesting to finally finish the building and watch that familiar pattern: "Okay, the project's over. Now what?" Here there are a zillion next projects; that's not a problem. What I've seen is my belief that once a project is done, then I can start living my life, then I can start being satisfied with my work, then I can relax; once the building is inspected, I will have

time to do all these fantasy projects that involve no one else, just me. But that never happens, because I step right back into the pattern of taking on the next big project. Of course, I could be responsible for the biggest project in the world, with a thousand things going on, and there's no reason I would need to tense up and leave the present moment in order to get through it.

Life can get very hard when I'm desperately trying to have control. For instance, I'll make a work plan for the week, and then Cheri will show up and everything changes. Suddenly, Tom is doing something Cheri would like done instead of what I wanted him to do. I ask Tony to do something, and he writes back that Cheri asked him to do something else. I say to myself, "Well, then, who's going to the dump? Why didn't she consult me? Doesn't she know the dump is only open on certain days?" I watch how I get so attached to how I think things should be, what I assume needs to get done. Eventually, I let go and realize, well, it will be a lot of fun next week to pile a double load of stuff on the truck and take it to the dump. (And it *was* fun.)

The work director job can involve writing notes to other monks, requests that something be done differently or reminders of certain guidelines. That is an important part of my practice. The purpose of the notes is simple: if in doing a task, you forgot something or you assumed something, the note points that out. Say your instructions were to chop carrots, and when you'd done that, you saw the soup pot on the stove, so you dumped the carrots in. Your assumption that the carrots belonged in the soup might not be correct, so you would receive a note asking you to follow instructions more carefully and not to assume anything outside the note. Or, if you didn't clean up the tools after finishing a task or you made a mess and left it, you might get a note reminding you that cleaning up is always part of the work assignment. On the surface, the note can look and feel like a reprimand, but it is only pointing out that our attention has wandered. We're here to do an awareness practice, we want to be as conscious as we can, and when we're not paying attention, we want to know it. The note is just a way of waking us up to many ways in which we're pulled around by our conditioning without realizing it.

On the writing end of the notes, the same assumptions and beliefs can be operating as on the receiving end. Namely, assuming that it's a reprimand, assuming that it means there's something wrong, that the person who gets the note is bad, that the person who writes the note has some authority and the person receiving the note is subject to that authority. I don't want people to see me as an authority. I don't want to reprimand people. I don't want to hurt people's feelings. I don't want people to feel bad. I want people to see me as a nice, supportive, kind person, so I have a lot of identity built up in my expectation of how the note will be received.

When my job is to bring something to someone's attention, and to do that in as neutral a way as possible—without apology, without excuse—that's very difficult if I'm tied up in believing that what they did was wrong or that if I write the note they will see me as an authority and not like me. I have to step beyond those beliefs to see, what are we here for? I want to offer to others the same thing I want for myself, which is assistance in this awareness practice. I don't really want to be liked, although my conditioning will tell me I do. And I don't really want to like anyone, not on a personality level, because what we share is something much deeper than that.

There are ways I can tell when a note I write isn't entirely neutral. How I react to the response of the person who receives the note may show that I had some string attached, an unstated desire for a specific outcome. Those strings can be positive or negative—the other person may be pleased or displeased—but it doesn't matter what their reaction is, it only matters that it is a sign to me that I was operating from my conditioning instead of from clarity.

I've used the word "neutral" but that may be misleading. It is not that there is no emotional component or that the response is bland and lifeless, not at all. Other words might be "clean" or "clear" or "without unfinished business." It means not leaving things in an unresolved state, internally or externally. I think of the phrase "leave not a trace." In this context that might mean that I don't want bits of unconscious conditioned feelings and beliefs clinging to those notes I write; unexamined, misunderstood bits of karmic stuff left for me or others to deal with later. Whatever conditioned patterns are not seen clearly in the moment and accepted for what they are seem to leave "traces" that can cause further suffering. I want to take all of myself into each moment, to be fully alive, rather than leaving fingernail tracks in the dirt as I desperately cling to my resistance while I'm being dragged along through life.

Writing notes on particular issues or to particular people can be a real challenge. Sometimes I just write the note and tack it on the board. Other times, I spend more time than I'd like to admit in rewrites; then I *know* there's something going on with me, there's some way in which I'm trying desperately to maintain a certain identity, often the identity of the model monk. Another uncomfortable situation can be writing a note asking someone not to do something that I do myself. Who likes being told not to leave tools lying around by someone who does that herself? *I* am always forgetting things, *I* often leave a mess—how dare *I* write this note asking someone else to meet standards that I don't meet? It's been helpful to see that that's totally beside the point. The point is that we assist each other in the process of becoming more conscious: seeing what we are not awake to, seeing how our actions affect others, seeing how we cling to our desires for comfort or acceptance. The bottom line is, whether I'm writing the notes or I'm getting the notes, this whole system is just a construct to help us become more aware.

What we don't do here is get a note and then write back an explanation or apology. Someone who receives a note saying, "Please clean up the paint brushes that were left outside" may want to write a note back saying, "I didn't leave those paint brushes there," or, "So-and-so told me to leave them," or whatever. But that would short-circuit the process of observing our conditioned responses.

On the work director's side, I've watched the struggle (in those extended rewrites) not to say things like, "Cheri said . . . ," or "Cheri's suggestion is . . .", trying to pin it on the *real* authority, trying to shift the blame for being a hardnose. You can see the temptation! It's the same on the receiving end: we restrain ourselves from that desperate impulse to say, "It's not my fault." And in doing that, we are able to see the underlying assumption that there's something wrong. Once we get beyond that, we can realize that all that's really going on with these notes is that we want to be aware of our mental processes, we want to be fully present to our experience.

Cheri helps me see assumptions I've made about what it's like to act in a conscious way. For instance, I can be very angry about something that another monk has done or not done. The issue needs to be addressed, but I want to maintain my identity as a nice, rational, compassionate, spiritual person, and by ego's definition, anger is excluded from that.

Let's say you have a habit of leaving the shower a mess. Anybody should know that's not a monkly thing to do [laughing]; you're supposed to clean up after yourself—"leave not a trace." But every time I go in the bathroom after you've taken a shower, the mat is soaking wet and in a wad on the floor, and hairs and soap scum are stuck all over the drain. Let's say this has been happening for quite a while, and I've tried to ignore it, but now I'm angry, resentful, sick of going into the bathroom and finding it a wreck when *I* have to take *my* shower. Somebody needs to tell Cheri about this! Then I think, "Why do *I* have to be the one to say something?"

In fact, there is nothing personal about cleaning up the hairs, there's nothing personal about telling Cheri about it, there's nothing personal about me and my shower. To continue to ignore it is not helpful to you or me or the monastic community or the strengthening of anyone's awareness practice. Getting angry isn't helpful. But I can use the energy I have about it to find a way of addressing it that is helpful—write it on the list of things to discuss with Cheri or whatever is appropriate—taking that energy as a signal for myself to pay closer attention and see what conditioned patterns are in play. One of the deepest patterns is to take it all personally, feeling, "This affects me, what should I do?" That's not necessary. What's going on is not about something personal between one individual and another, it's just the interplay of conditioned behavior patterns, some of which revolve around me and some around you. But asking you to clean up after yourself doesn't require me to be mad at you or think you're a bad person. One of Cheri's gifts as a teacher is that she sees clearly that a person's conditioned behavior has nothing to do with who that person truly is.

In a guidance appointment, Cheri and I had this great discussion about monks practicing as peers. We are peers when we are not separate, so in essence we are always peers; it's the illusion of separateness that makes us think that we are not. Let's say I fail to follow a guideline.

It's your job to notice that and respond, and maybe you sense that I'm acting from urgency or fear or anger or some other conditioning. Are we peers in that moment? I have a belief system—which is being uprooted—that says we are not peers then, that there's somebody conscious and somebody unconscious, and we know who is the better person. But neither one of us has to believe that we're not connected. When I'm not paying attention, when I'm identified with my conditioning, when I'm suffering, the chances are that I believe we are separate. But *you* don't have to believe it; you can know that we are peers. You can just look at me and think, "I know, Mary, I've been there. I'm sorry for you, honey. You can come home any time you want. But I'm not going out in the cold with you." So, if we want to interact on the level of being peers, it is important that we have a commitment to being responsible for our sense of connectedness. The basis of our agreement is that we will remember that we are not separate—even when we get lost in conditioning.

Cheri has said that as long as the student remains the student, the teacher will remain the teacher, but when the student-teacher relationship is no longer needed, the hierarchical relationship dissolves. At some point, we need to take full responsibility for our own practice. That doesn't mean that there isn't benefit from being around someone who has more experience. But the hierarchy in the relationship is no longer necessary.

For whatever reason, I have a certain propensity for this life; living with other people who do this practice is helpful to me. I want to know how to be with people without assuming separation. A good place to start might be interacting with people who have the same desire—the desire to end suffering, and the willingness to work toward that. Generally, we think of peers as people who have the same abilities or credentials, but here we are peers because we have that same desire.

Compassion and the
Paradox of No Escape

Someone who enters a monastery with the idea that life's difficulties can be left behind, no less than someone who seeks refuge in addiction of whatever sort, is bound to experience disillusionment, since there is no escape from oneself. But once we acknowledge our predicament—that we suffer needlessly in self-imposed prisons of confusion and fear—escape is no longer an issue: acceptance transforms suffering into compassion.

When I interviewed Lois, she had been at the Monastery for only three weeks, at which point the world of nature, still very much "other," presented serious challenges. "One of the things they don't do here is kill bugs," she said, admitting that she was not "a camper." It seemed to me that Lois had consciously committed to living in a place where she knew there was no illusion of escape and to the process of bringing clarity and compassion to that situation.

> The first week, I was waking up in the middle of the night terrified. Part of it is being cut off from civilization. I love to read the newspaper and know what's going on; the people I lived with [Catholic Workers] are very political, and we talked a lot about real world stuff. Reading the paper made me feel like part of something larger, and now all of

a sudden that doesn't matter anymore, like I'm not alive and no one cares. It's like dying, in a way. Maybe in a year I'll break the addiction, or replace it with an addiction to silence. Meanwhile, things are very busy here, and I have too much to do to be upset.

[Each day] you get these little notes giving you your work assignment and directions about how to do it. I'm working on sanding and finishing redwood boards for doors, work I've never done and would never have any desire to do. And weeding—physical work. I don't feel that I'm very good at it. Which is all, as they say, okay.

I really like eating and cleaning up in silence. I came here without a clue about how things worked, where the dishes go, and so on. Phyl showed me at first by pointing: "There's a towel," meaning, dry the dishes. I was tense not only because I knew I'd do something wrong, but also because I knew I wasn't supposed to be thinking that way about it. But no one tells you if you do anything wrong, and no one tells you if you do anything right. You just do it. It's so interesting—I can walk out of the kitchen feeling as if I did everything wrong, and yet no one said a word to me. It becomes very clear how much of what we are thinking comes from within ourselves. Here no one is criticizing me, so I have to recognize where that sense of being wrong comes from and deal with it in myself. I notice that when I am able to feel all right about something within myself, even if criticism does come from outside, it doesn't really bother me that much.

Rather than escaping into a fantasy of something we are not, but merely by being more completely, more consciously who we are, we can dissolve the barrier that defines the self as separate from everything else. For example, a familiar experience to meditators is the automatic extension of compassion beyond the boundaries of the self.

Let's say that, like Lois, you suffer from a fear of spiders, and you've just moved to a place where spiders seem to be everywhere.

Meditation will help you get to know your fear: with a calm mind, you can examine its nature, its origin, its effects on your body and behavior. You will also see your conditioned reactions to fear, which commonly include the desire to change one's circumstances ("I've got to get away from here"), along with blame and guilt ("Why don't they clean the corners more carefully?" and, the other side of the duality, "I should just get over this"). Once you have seen your suffering clearly and deeply, compassion arises spontaneously, and with an interesting after-effect: the same suffering in others is met with the same compassion. The next time you notice yourself feeling that someone else should just get over their fear, you will be less likely to dismiss their experience, because you can guess that it is very much like your own.

In her 1992 interview, Phyllis described how most if not all of the work toward finding compassion comes in finding it for oneself.

Acceptance is actually not a big deal, and it's not some airy-fairy thing—it's simply allowing whatever is, including all this human stuff that we say we shouldn't do, we shouldn't think, we shouldn't be. The reason acceptance seems hard is that there's a stretch of uncharted territory, and to move into that requires faith. It's like the moment of letting go of one trapeze and flying through mid-air before you catch the next one. When I have been willing to accept all that was there, I could feel the faith stretching from one point to the next, feel it growing.

The whole process of allowing everything to come, no matter what category—confusion, misery, anger—that's something I've learned in the past few months. What I'm talking about is out and out suffering, being totally identified with ego. I would say to myself, "I shouldn't be miserable, I hate being miserable, I want to be happy." But Cheri's guidance was to just wallow in the misery. So I did, and I'm finally experiencing on a more subtle level what it is to allow things to be. To be extremely angry, knowing that I'm in a process that will lead away from anger, or to be extremely miserable, knowing that I'm letting it be there so that that part of me can be healed and I won't need to identify with it—it works. I'm actually eager for my next bout of misery, because it gives me more material to practice with.

During a recent period when I was caught in anger, I didn't talk to anybody about it for three weeks, because I wanted it to build up to a point where it would burn itself out. At times when I felt intense anger in my body, I would tell myself, it's okay, I can be with this, I can experience this and it will be all right. I can go punch things, and that doesn't make me a bad person; I can go meditate, and that doesn't make me a good person. Complete acceptance of anger may mean going off by yourself and punching things or having imaginations of what you want to do to people—and *not* judging yourself for it, not assuming that this makes you a bad person.

To be able to do that was a new experience for me. It meant accepting things I'd never seen in myself; I'd never allowed myself to be angry that way. Then, sitting in meditation, which I did a lot, got me in touch with the peace and compassion in myself, and I knew that all this other stuff was me spinning my wheels, me letting it out.

I had a sense that I was going through something important, that this was actually a blessing. And I was determined to let it unfold, to allow everything to be there, to stick with it, stick with it, stick with it—just the way you do in sitting meditation. Along with feeling very angry and miserable, I would feel joy, because some part of me was so happy that I was allowing this to happen, this particular movement toward freedom.

Now, when other circumstances arise similar to what triggered that original reaction, now I can just go to that experience of compassion within myself. In the past, I tried to use my mind to fix that fearful or angry part, to talk it out of feeling that way, telling it that everything is really okay, when it isn't. When I drop that and be with whatever is going on, when I allow it to be whatever it is, not denying or negating it, that's compassion. Then it dissolves or relaxes, although it still may come back later.

The more I am able to do that with the different aspects of myself, the more I am experiencing life. And the more accepting and open I am with my own fear or anger or misery, the more compassionate I can be in those same areas with other people. If I notice ways in which my compassion is not there for others, those are the areas that are not yet acceptable to me. So, I can use the very experience of lacking compassion to become aware of ways in which I have not brought compassion to myself, and every time I extend the compassion within myself, I naturally extend it toward others. Either way, the buck stops here—that old Buddhist saying.

In fact, the self can be viewed as the raw material each of us is given to work with. Whatever compassion we can discover for our own fears and failings and foolishness seems to multiply effortlessly toward others, and the more intimate our relationship with our own suffering, the more connection we feel with everyone and everything.

Thus, the usual injunction to be "unselfish" gets turned inside out: first one must look inward, to oneself, bringing compassion to whatever is found there. That very self is seen then to be no different from other selves, and there arises a distinct feeling that "we are all in this together." In this way, the "no-self" of Buddhism (or "no separate self") gently manifests in our awareness, slipping bit by bit from abstract concept to lived experience.

Through this process, the solitary monk becomes one with the world.

◇

Ann

Ann has practiced with Cheri for ten years. She spent a year at the Monastery in 1994-95, and at the time of this interview, 1998, she had just arrived for a second year.

I first went to the Zen Center when somebody invited me to a workshop. We did a centering exercise, and when Cheri said, "See if you can be in the space between the thoughts," I began crying and crying. I told Cheri I felt as if I could cry forever. She said, "Be my guest. You can go outside. I think the record is an hour."

I was committed from that moment. What impressed me most was Cheri's fearlessness. Nothing could bother her; everything was perfectly okay, and I was aware of that in her presence. I also knew that Cheri didn't want anything from me, didn't care, in a way, whether I came back or not. With other things I'd tried, there was a sense of their wanting something or your being a bad person if you didn't go along with them and their way. At the Zen Center, there was none of that. And I perceived that clearly in the single day of that workshop.

I began signing up for everything offered at the Zen Center and going on retreats. At one point, Cheri said it would be a good gift for people to give themselves to commit to a year at the Monastery. Everything in me said, yes, that's what I want to do. But it was about another two years until my life circumstances were such (and until I got up the courage) that I could quit my job and come here for a year.

When I arrived, only Phyl and Cameron were here. When I'd been here about a month, I noticed myself looking at the two of them and thinking, "I could never live here." Of course, I *was* living here. That was a very good example for me of how the voices in our heads are not something we need to believe. Had I not been living here, had I just been on a weekend retreat, for example, and that voice had come up, I probably would have believed it and gone off on all the reasons why I could never live here and what a horrible place it was, and so on. But I caught it, saw it as just a voice, because, in fact, I was indeed living here. Sometimes egocentricity exposes itself when we're paying attention, and then we can see through it. If we're not paying attention, we tend to believe it. So, all the more reason to pay attention!

That summer it was *so* hot, and we were digging ditches in densely rocky ground in 110-degree weather. It sounds horrible, but in the moment, your attitude can just be, "What's the next thing to do?" It's dig the ditch, and you do it. The ditches were for electrical cables from the greenhouse and generator to the kitchen. We had laid pipes and run the wires through and filled in the ditches with dirt, and the electrician came to check it all. He said we didn't have enough wiring, and it would all have to be dug up and done again. So, we were ready to dig it up and start over; that was just the next thing to do. Nobody had a reaction like, "Oh, my god, what a disaster, how can this be?" Well, maybe we did internally, but since this is a silent environment, we didn't say anything. The electrician was amazed. He said he'd never seen anybody who greeted that kind of bad news with complete calm.

Another time when it was terribly hot, I had to go out in the car, and I noticed a voice in me saying, "I am so hot. I can't stand this!" Now, I had the air conditioning on in the car, so in that moment, I was not hot. Normally, when we hear a voice like that, we agree. "Yeah, it's really hot, this place sucks." But it's possible to hear the voice and question it: "Is that so?" That was a wonderful experience: hearing the voice, checking to see if it accurately reflected my experience, discovering that it didn't, and realizing that everything was really all right. We miss our life experience when we listen to the voices in our heads and believe them, without checking in with our body and our senses. We talk about living from the neck up—that's the life of ego. The only way we can reclaim our whole lives is to add that process of checking in with ourselves to see what we're actually experiencing on the sensory level.

Cameron told a wonderful story about her hermitage being filled with mosquitoes that were biting her, and finally she couldn't stand it any more, and she grabbed a book and started to whack one of them. Then she looked at the book, and it was Thich Nhat Hanh's *Being Peace*. Having heard a lot of stories like that, when I was cutting wood and mosquitoes were biting me, I tried to "be peace" and accept them and see that it was my reaction to them and not the mosquitoes themselves—all those things people say. But, in fact, I hated it. Finally, I couldn't take any more, and I wished instant death to every mosquito on the planet; I imagined killing them all. And at that moment, I was having a good time. I was no longer trying to be the good Zen student, trying to be what I heard in those stories, trying and failing to find compassion and be one with the mosquitoes. To be able to be one with the part of me that hated mosquitoes and wanted them dead, that dissolved the resistance. Then I didn't have any problem being there. It was *trying to have it not be a problem* that created such a problem.

◇

Spiritual practice is a process of growing up, of taking responsibility for growing up. In that sense, I was a lot younger when I was here the first time. I felt a certain rebelliousness against the schedule, like a kid saying, "Why do I have to do this if they don't have to?" And there was the constant fear—am I doing it right? what's the rule? who's watching me?—that makes life so hard. When we come to the Monastery, we attempt to do everything right and be good, to be our best conditioned selves. (That is, of course, until we can't take the pressure any more and we move to the other side of the duality and decide to act out, be "bad" in some way.) Cheri says most people at the Monastery are trying to be good instead of being open to life.

I am just beginning to see that, and it's so sad, because it keeps us stuck. Working so hard to be good just ensures ego's continued existence. It's like that saying, "Enlightenment is as easy as falling off a log, and we're all trying so hard to stay on."

Someone said recently that she's just now coming to understand that the Monastery isn't a punitive place. I can see how people might experience it that way, because if we're living from those beliefs of egocentric conditioning—wanting to be good, wanting to be right, putting all our energy into being good/right—then any time we get information that conflicts with those beliefs, any time we are jarred awake out of our conditioning, out of the false reality we've created for ourselves, we can experience that as punitive. "How can someone ask me to be mindful, when I'm working so hard to be good?" But if our interest is to see how we cause ourselves to suffer, it's not punitive, it's just an opportunity to see.

For example, I'd just taken a shower (at that time there were only the outdoor shower and outhouses), and I really had to go to the bathroom. My choice was either to break a guideline by going to the bathroom in the bushes or break a guideline by running through the bushes straight to the outhouse, rather than going around the long way on the path. I made a beeline through the bushes to the outhouse. And I got a note saying, "Please stay on the established trails." I could have created suffering for myself by taking an attitude like, "That person is so mean, watching me all the time, just waiting for me to make a mistake." But that person is just doing their job of pointing out the guidelines, which is a way of saying, please be conscious. Part of me was annoyed, but then I thought, well, of my two choices, I probably made the better one, and it wasn't necessary to explain that. I could simply feel, "Thanks for the reminder," because it's for my own practice. The point is to see how I cause myself to suffer.

It's an intense path. I get the image of a roller-coaster ride, sometimes. It's not a popular journey. You don't get a lot of reinforcement from the world. I don't know what causes me to keep on with it, because the pull is so great to do anything but this.

During the last three years, when I wasn't living here, I worked hard to include spiritual practice as a core part of my life. Here at the Monastery there seems to be a certain energy that's calibrated with the rhythm of life, and it's very peaceful. But out in the world— I went from the Monastery to a start-up company in Silicon Valley— it was culture shock. Here we are trained to see that if you're operating from a sense of urgency, you are operating out of egocentric conditioning and you need to look at that and let it go. Out in the world, if you're *not* driven by urgency, there's a belief that you're not working hard enough. On a superficial level, I could say that when I was living out in the world, I did get caught up in that rhythm of life. But at a deep level, having been here for a year had an effect. In many situations, I was able to find the strength to go with my heart, against all the voices of conditioning.

Last November I decided to come back. I'd been thinking about it for a year and a half. I know this is what's important to me, but I also wondered if I was moving toward it as an escape. I talked to Cheri about it, and she said, "It *is* an escape—an escape from suffering." It felt important to me to take time to make the decision, to sit with it, to show myself that I could be in the world, to be sure it wasn't an escape from that.

Being here now, I have the sense that there's enough time, there's enough space, there's enough love—*there is enough love.* Any time I'm present, I can have that experience. Now there's a certain resting in the schedule. I feel that I am really doing monastic training this time, and there's much more gratitude for this place. This time (so far, anyway), it's like being on the most wonderful—well, the word that comes to me doesn't feel entirely right, but—vacation. I get to breathe fresh, clean air; yesterday I got to climb a tree and get onto a roof and put plastic on it, and I was feeling, "This is so much

fun!" Walking to my hermitage at night and seeing a full moon—
it seems as if every moment is a gift I can delight in.

There's a quotation from Bunan [17th-century Zen master] we're
fond of repeating around here. "Die while you're alive and be absolutely
dead. Then do whatever you want: it's all good." Imagine a situation
in which something has come to an end: let's say you've resigned
from a job, you're working those last two weeks, and there's such a
sense of freedom about it—you can do what you need to do and say
what you need to say, because there's no fear of consequences.
Wouldn't it be great if we could do that with our lives? Die now, then
live the rest of your life as if you're already dead—no worry about

retirement, no worry about anything! You can just drop your karmic conditioning, drop your annoying habits, all the things that cause you to suffer—*whoosh,* let it all go, and just be here, enjoying the moment.

◇

I think it's important for people to realize that they do themselves a grave disservice if they choose to practice or not practice based on who is sitting on the cushion as teacher. It's not about who's sitting on the teacher's cushion, it's about who's sitting on *your* cushion. I remember a meeting at the Zen Center years ago when someone said to Cheri, "I don't want to come to a workshop unless you're the one leading it." Cheri leaned forward and said, pointing to herself, "It's not about this person." And I got it: spiritual practice is about the practice, not the teacher. This training involves becoming aware of your internal process, cutting through your conditioning, bringing compassionate awareness to whatever is going on. Someone else may encourage and assist you, but you are the only one who can end your suffering. You are the only one who knows intimately what you have experienced and what all those abandoned parts of you need in order to be healed. Of course, when we first start practicing, we don't know we know. And so we have a teacher and a *sangha* to help us "exercise our compassion muscles," you might say, until we realize for ourselves, "Yes, I am capable of ending suffering, and not only that, I am the only one who can do it."

I used to argue with the friend who brought me to the Zen Center originally about how important it is to find the right teacher. I'd say, "The teacher doesn't matter, you have to do this yourself, it has nothing to do with the teacher. You could practice with a turnip, and if you practice sincerely, you'll see what you need to see." Then when I was at the Monastery, this friend wrote me a letter saying, "I don't think Cheri's the right teacher for you, you need to find another teacher." That riled me up. I wrote her back and said, "You know, you were right after all: the teacher is important."

In fact, there's this paradoxical middle ground where the teacher doesn't matter and the teacher matters. I would have come to the Monastery to practice even if Cheri were not going to be here for this year. But there's also a sense of wanting to stay with the path I'm on and wanting to continue working with her as my teacher.

I'm wary about adulation of the teacher; there's something dangerous about that. Which is not to say that I don't adulate Cheri. But it's clear to me that I have to take complete responsibility for my spiritual practice. I'm very grateful that I am able to practice within the structure that Cheri has created, and with that gratitude, there's a sense of wanting to give something back.

Cheri is training people now—as guestmaster or work director or spiritual guide, in whatever role—by asking them what they would do in a given situation, allowing them to look inside and see how they would respond, then letting them know if they are on target, so to speak. It's helping each of us find our own center, so we can act from that. So, when Cheri talks about training other people to be teachers, I want to be as supportive as I can as they step into that position, to be supportive for them as a student, just as they support me in my training.

Freedom and the Paradox of Nothing To Do

"Doing" as directed by egocentricity is effortful, driven, draining, whereas responding to whatever arises in each moment is acting in freedom; nothing is required in the way of tension or strain. In a sense, nothing at all is required, except, as Cheri puts it, "showing up." That is, we can bring our attention so completely into the present moment that each next thing in life simply unfolds, with each of us taking our natural part in the whole, effortlessly.

This is exemplified for me in Tom's discussion of the building process. From the time the land was graded, Tom carried a lot of responsibility, since he was the only person at the Monastery with much experience in construction and woodworking. Yet when he spoke about the work, it was always within the context of spiritual practice, about action flowing from awareness, about "listening to the building."

> What I want from my training now is to learn to let life live me. It's like this building—we let it build itself. It can be as simple as this: you have a board to fasten to the wall, and you have to decide whether to use nails or screws. Which do we have? Well, we have this kind of nail and this kind of screw. Do we have a drill? Yes. Do we have a drill bit? Yes. So, we can go either way; we are still in the realm of

possibility. How do we want it to look? Do we care whether there's a big hunky nail showing? Yes. So we decide on the screw, put it in, and the board cracks. That means the board wants to be pre-drilled. We pre-drill it and put the screw in, and the head doesn't go flush all the way, so the board wants the screw to be counter-sunk. That's how the building talks to you. That's how the building got built: we figured it out as we went along. It emerged as a product of a practice. That was the only way it could have taken shape.

I had expected (hoped, to be honest) that Tom would describe how, during his first stay at the Monastery, he made the six-paned casement windows that are one of the most beautiful features of the building, and how he taught that skill to others. I wanted to hear him talk about concentrated mindfulness, the attentive care that is developed in meditation, how hard it was to get the windows right, the drama of his struggles and failures. Tom didn't see it in those terms. So I asked him to tell me what it was like when the forest fire approached: what if all the windows he had built at that point had been destroyed? He said they would have started over, made new windows, no problem; it would simply have taken more time. That attitude impressed me as being the opposite of my own approach: filling time with doing, then feeling frustrated, sometimes frantic, because there's so little time.

In a place where there is so much to be done, where work is an integral part of spiritual training, it would seem absurd to speak of "nothing to do." Yet the daily schedule can have the effect of dissolving the burden of work, it seems, and after spending even short periods at the Monastery, some people find it so freeing that they establish a semi-monastic schedule when they return to their regular lives. When I was there completing the interviews for this book, I was prepared to follow the monks' schedule, because I had heard that that would be required. I expected it to be grueling, confining, but that I would be stoic and in the end feel virtuous. Instead, Cheri told me that I could do whatever I wanted to with my time. No doubt she knew that I would find dealing with nothing to do far more difficult than meeting a schedule.

In fact, I did follow the monks' schedule, by choice, which allowed me to experience the freedom of not thinking ahead about what I was going to do next, not drumming up activities to fill in empty spaces, but doing only what was right there in each moment to be done. "Doing the next thing" and "being lived by life" and "nothing to do"— all those expressions point toward an ease of being that is one of the fruits of monastic practice.

◇

A.

In college in the 1960s, A. was a political science student in moccasins and bellbottoms, searching for ultimate truth. Krishnamurti seemed to have it, but when she finished reading his book, she said, "the discontent and searching was still in me." For thirteen years, she worked in the alternative community, then in 1986 was offered a job at Southern Dharma Retreat Center. In the process of considering whether or not to take the job, she attended a retreat led by Cheri. "I questioned it all," A. recalled, "trying to disprove whatever she said, while part of me desperately wanted to accept it." A. did take the job at Southern Dharma and later spent several periods at the Monastery.

When I had the opportunity to take a sabbatical, I came out here to the Monastery for a month. I found it spiritually deepening and physically rewarding. But the cynic in me was also alive and well, and I left saying to myself, "Well, I don't have to do that again, because I can see certain problems with the place." I was looking through lenses that reveal flaws, because if I find enough flaws, then I can say no to this experience; I can say, "This isn't it, either." That feels comfortable, familiar; again I can be the loner and the idealist.

Later, I decided to come back to the Monastery for another month. That was more of a spiritual experience, because I was more open, I allowed myself to just be a monk instead of a critical observer on the sidelines.

Ever since childhood, when I read a book about two children having a garden, gardening had been something I wanted to do; pictures from that book are still vivid in my mind. So when I wrote about wanting to come to the Monastery the second time, I asked if I could work in the garden, and the response was yes. It turned out to be such a great experience that before I left at the end of that month, I asked if I could return for a longer time and be the regular

Zen gardener. Cheri said, "Sure, come back and be the gardener." Wow, I thought, a dream come true, everything I've always wanted. So I returned yet again, and this time I'm here for six months.

There are days when I think, why ever leave? This is a beautiful place, I've got my hermitage under an unbelievable oak tree, it's near the garden, I have my own outhouse, there's scrumptious food. I'm meditating daily and doing work I love. What more could I want?

Still, I find I drag myself around with myself, so to speak. I'm doing the garden exactly the way I have always done my work: driving myself. Nothing I do is ever big enough or good enough; I have to do *more*. I couldn't be content to restore the existing garden, I had to dig new garden plots, and on and on. No one else has any expectations that I do these things. Phyl might mention that the tomatoes need more water, but if we didn't get one tomato out of this garden, it wouldn't be a problem for anybody except *me*. My dissatisfied ego puts those ideas in my head: we could do this, we could do that—I have this "Zen-dried tomatoes" idea now. Why not? Let's do it! I leave a note for the work director and get no response. Then I realize, that's my ego again.

Krishnamurti said if you question everything, you'll see that all these conditioned beliefs have been fed into you, that it's a brainwashing system. I understand that on an intellectual level, but now I am beginning to see how difficult it is, how deep the conditioning goes. I find it difficult to disengage from the attitude of "I have to . . .", even though everyone around me is encouraging me to look at how I am the one requiring myself to work in this mode. The purpose of this job is for my spiritual practice, to show me *how* I do things. That's clear to me, but I'm muddled about how to change it—or rather how to accept it, because it's only in acceptance that it will change.

Hours go by when I'm caught up in my own struggles: this is so hard, why am I doing this? Right now I'm struggling with the

irrigation system, which isn't working. Why do we even try to grow vegetables in a summer with no rainfall? Why don't we grow something easy, like aloe vera plants? *Why am I doing this?* I have the hardest time just relaxing into enjoying life. I feel I've got to work hard, if I don't work hard, I'm slacking off, then I won't get approval. And yet I *want* to slack off. But I don't. Round and round the mind rolls.

A number of times it has struck me when I'm out in the garden, "*This is* my life." It's not like being in the monastery isn't real life, and I'll have my life when I leave here. This is *it,* right now. When I'd been here only a few weeks, I was digging beds, which is hard work. One day I said to myself, "Okay, this is your last day on earth . . . ," and immediately my mind said, "Well, then, get out of here!" I wanted to indulge myself: go to the ocean, drink good coffee, go shopping, all those distractions. But I saw that for what it was, and what I really wanted to do on my last day was dig the garden bed. So, that's what I did, and I enjoyed it. I hardly suffered that day.

Phyl helped me realize some things about my constant questioning of authority. Something came out in a group discussion that I perceived as a major flaw in how things are run here, and I commented on it. That night I went back to my hermitage figuring I'd just pack and leave, because I didn't want to stay since I'd exposed this place as operating on less than the ultimate truth. But Phyl pointed out that none of us are here because we've found ultimate truth—we're here to learn what keeps us from the truth. That voice in me quieted, and I've been able to examine how I question authority. I've been misled by authorities, but the problem is that I've looked outside myself and wanted to believe that what others tell me is the truth. Now I am seeing that truth is not out there, it's within my own heart.

Aside from questioner and cynic, there are other roles I can't disengage from. Sometimes I just want to say or hear something funny. I'll be doing the dishes, and a bowl will strike a lid just right and sound like a bell, and I'll do it again and again so I can get everybody's attention and make them laugh. Maybe I am projecting it, but there seems to be a somberness here. I miss having time for giggling, acting crazy, just having fun. When I leave the Monastery to do an errand—go to the airport to pick somebody up or to the neighbor's to get llama manure for the garden—I want to be more myself, not just some distant, noninvolved being. We've talked about it in group discussions, how you can be personable and present and still not get involved. When I get in my car and go out, there's a sense of freedom I experience that I don't feel in this environment. In group discussions we laugh and joke, but afterwards we're back to the seriousness. I'm not saying it's the environment; I know it's within me. It would be interesting to look more deeply into that, but I'm still holding on to my ideas that there should be more humor, more smiling. In my monastery, each morning we'll look each other directly in the eyes and smile.

The fact that Cheri has stepped back enough to allow us all to be our own teachers is one of the most important things she's offered. The teaching pervades our lives; it is a constant reminder of what our hearts are searching for. We lose the way because the voices in our minds are louder than the still voice of our hearts, so we keep following egocentricity down the road of conditioning. The guide is standing over on a nice little path saying, "Hey, it's over here! You want to come over here and take a walk?" "No, I'm busy on my path: the road to success and dissatisfaction . . . ." When there's going to be guidance with Cheri, there's a tendency to think, "Oh, great, the big answer is going to come!" But I can be by myself out in the garden, paying attention, being willing to be aware, and teaching can come to me through that.

Here at the Monastery is a group of people living in sincerity and compassion and willingness to look for that ultimate desire, to satisfy the yearning of our hearts—which doesn't happen many places. This place is set up for one purpose, to end suffering. It's hard to believe; it seems not real, not of this planet, but here it is.

I tell myself that I'm being denied things here, and everything will be okay when I leave and can freely get good coffee when I want it and don't have to drink instant. And I suspect that the day when I drive out of here, I'll be saying, "I wish I could go back to the Monastery. I wish I were driving in the other direction."

Happiness

In these interviews, laughter often punctuates accounts of the dire, dismal, and desperate in spiritual practice. Indeed, difficulty comes to be welcomed, because it presents yet another opportunity to *see through* the mental conditioning that produces the suffering, to recognize the absurdity of it all.

I wonder if that laughter marks a shift, however momentary, to egolessness, a quick passage into the blessed state in which one is no longer confined within the "small mind" of our conditioning. In Zen, "gateless gate" refers to that shift. Once you are on the other side, you realize that there was no gate after all, no barrier, no personhood to be damaged by ideas of appearance or competence or status or even pain. Indeed, the whole notion becomes laughable. Sometimes Cheri provokes laughter merely by calling attention to what is happening here and now, releasing us from the constricted perspective of egocentricity to the infinite joy of participating in all that is.

Joy is frequently mentioned in the monks' accounts of their lives, though more often the word "freedom" is used. "Happiness" seems harder to say, perhaps because it has long carried a stigma of triviality, but also, I suspect, because so many of us, if we look closely, hold a subtle fear of happiness. Not the happiness of chocolate (or travel or money or romance or achievement) but an abiding and indestructible well-being: the very possibility can seriously threaten our ideas of who we are and what we need to do in life.

Buddhism has always addressed happiness implicitly, since the Buddha's great discovery was that there is an end to suffering. In our tendency to cling to the safety of what we know, however, we tend to misinterpret Buddhism as being "about suffering." Today, more and more books on Buddhism are turning up with the "h"-word in the titles. My favorite is Robert Thurman's *Inner Revolution: Life, Liberty, and the Pursuit of Real Happiness,* in which he asserts that the point of the Buddha's teachings—indeed, the purpose of all life— is to find happiness, and that monasteries are educational institutions dedicated to that goal.

Monastic training dispels the illusion that happiness lies in getting our own way. Monks willingly give up having their own way, which, as most of us know (and repeatedly forget), offers only fleeting satisfaction. Instead, monks learn how to allow themselves to "be lived" by something beyond the limits of the self, beyond the dualities that normally drive our choices: good/bad, like/dislike, love/hate, self/other.

The happiness of chocolate is illusory and ephemeral; it is the illusion of salvation harnessed to the sensation of a moment. Learning to live fully in the present, which happens through meditation, means developing the ability to experience every moment. The happiness of chocolate is here and then it's gone. The deep happiness of this practice endures. Dharma takes root in our hearts and grows. To me, the monks in this book are visible signs of that living process.

◇

Dave

Dave spent most of his twenties living alone, trying to find a meaningful way of life outside conventional expectations. At the point when he realized that his efforts weren't working, he encountered this spiritual practice and is now in his second year at the Monastery.

I'd always read a lot, and I knew about Buddhism from an intellectual point of view, although I never expected that I would become involved in it. But when I met some people who meditated and had a weekly sitting group, I started going. One of the people in the group had been to a retreat with Cheri in North Carolina, and she suggested that we go to the next one, and several of us did.

I had a very profound experience there. I'm not sure what I saw, but it was something like a possibility that I hadn't perceived before. I had been trying to find ways to avoid doing, and finally here was something I could do. Basically, I stepped aside from my thoughts and experienced disidentification [from ego] for the first time in a conscious way. It was dramatic, frightening, a huge rush—and a gigantic switch in who I believed I was. I'd always thought I was whatever was going on my head, and I realized suddenly—very suddenly, from one minute to the next—that I am something else. That there is something in me that is not all these opinions and assumptions about who I think I am, something softer and more friendly and happy. And that was a very, very interesting experience.

After that, things began opening up for me inside. I became addicted to meditation, and I began thinking about coming here to the Monastery. I spent six months hiking on the Appalachian Trail, and I thought when I finished that, I'd come here.

Instead, I tried one last time to make my life work, taking a different approach. Living more or less alone in the woods had become unproductive, a dead end, and I decided to move to town, get a job like everybody else, make friends, and be happy. It didn't work at all. It seemed like every door was closed. Couldn't find a job, didn't make friends, had an awful time.

I spent so long looking for a job that another retreat with Cheri came around before I found one. So, I thought I'd go see Cheri again, since I'd had such a good experience with her before. On the first day of the retreat, in my guidance appointment I explained to Cheri that I'd decided not to come to the Monastery. In about five minutes, she had demolished the whole defense I'd built around that. I came out of guidance thinking, "Oh, my gosh, I guess I'm going to the Monastery." She didn't try to talk me into it or even suggest that it might be a good thing for me to do; she just pointed out what was obviously going on: I was defending myself out of fear, trying to protect myself from something I really wanted.

The fear was partly just because it was unknown, I suppose. But I think there was some hidden sense—how should I say this? What I was afraid of is what has actually happened! I had no clue as to how it worked before I came here. I didn't know that I wouldn't get to have my own way; I didn't know I'd be confronted at every turn by the ways I cause myself to suffer. I don't know what I thought, but a couple of months later I was here. That was almost a year ago.

I just returned yesterday after spending two months away visiting friends and family, so I'm freshly back from the conditioned world. I had a lot of preconceptions about what it would be like to leave here after nine months. I imagined that in a very short time, I would become totally unconscious, even that I would be swept away by something more powerful than I am and forget what I had learned here and maybe never come back. Right before I left, I decided that I did want to come back, and I made that commitment to Cheri to make sure it happened, to have an anchor here.

Actually, during those two months away, nothing dramatic happened. I'd been there only a couple of hours when I remembered what it's like in that world, and I remembered why I was at the Monastery, and I was ready to come back here right away. But my return ticket was for two months later, so I had that time to fill. It turned out to be very productive, and fun, too. As I expected, I did gradually start buying in to my conditioning, and I got to watch how that happens. But there was a foundation of self-acceptance and a feeling that everything is okay.

I did *everything* to be unconscious: I avoided meditation, I watched TV, I listened to the radio, I ran my mouth—I did everything I possibly could to avoid paying attention, and it didn't work. Oh, I was largely unconscious; even at the Monastery I'm largely unconscious. But there was something that hadn't been there before that was to be counted on, some acceptance. Toward the end of the two months, I was feeling very heavy, having trouble getting out of bed, life was becoming too serious, and I could tell that if I didn't come back here, that acceptance would erode over time.

I also had preconceptions about what it would be like to return here, that it would be hard, which it is. But as soon as I got back, I started feeling light again, feeling that this is where I belong. My big sense from the whole experience is that there is nothing for me out there, really. Not for the true me. During that two months I tried a lot of things. I tried everything I could in that short amount of time, and nothing was satisfying, nothing made me feel the way I feel when I'm here and don't have anything but me, my own friendship.

Being here is hard only from ego's perspective. It's like being a kid again: you get bossed around, you can't make any decisions, you can't go anywhere, you don't have any friends, you can't take yourself out to eat, can't do anything nice for yourself in the normal way. And everywhere you turn, there are guidelines that point out where you have gone unconscious.

It can seem brutal, but in reality it's not, because the focus of those guidelines is to help me to wake up. If someone points out to me that I'm asleep, or I point it out to myself, I suffer a lot over that, because it's like being caught in something. Ego is solidified around a certain way of being that I don't want to give up, and if I'm forced to give it up, that feels hard, like a tearing away. But what I get in return for that is learning to be free of the need to have those identities and the need to solidify around certain ideas about myself. I get to be a friend to myself and to experience self-acceptance.

A lot of people have a preconception that life at a monastery is serious; I guess people associate silence with seriousness. But we're practicing how to be happy here. Here, there is hope. It makes life seem full of possibility, and when you have that hope it's easy to be cheerful and lighthearted and to accept things as they come. When you're identified with life instead of suffering, doors open. Even practically, things happen for you, it seems like. Here there is continual opening up, exploration, having new kinds of experiences that you never expected or imagined or knew existed.

It happens many times a day in small ways. For example, first thing in the morning, I often feel some panic about being here. From ego's point of view, this is the craziest place on earth to be. It takes me a while to pull it together. Without the support of the environment here and this practice, I might carry that experience of panic through the whole day; it might become my identity for that day, or weeks or months or years even. There's something safe in that panic; I don't have to open myself up, I can stay closed, I don't have to risk being happy, I don't have to let go of who I think I am. But here it's impossible to stay in that panic because there's nothing to do but pay attention. And the incentive is huge to pay attention because you either pay attention or you're miserable. The more you're successful in paying attention, the more you experience that cheerfulness and lightheartedness. If I feel that panicky sort of way and then start paying attention to it, eventually it shifts, and then I experience something else. Like fun.

This morning I've been having fun in my work. I haven't done my job for these two months that I've been away, so it's been fun getting back into it. Probably around mid-afternoon I'll start feeling some heaviness, then something will happen, and it will shift again. Because I'm paying attention, I'll be able to open up to life and experience the satisfaction and contentment that's available to me all the time, which sometimes I'm not able to see.

Meditation provides a way to be in touch with that part of me that I discovered at that first retreat and that I suspected, I think, before that. It's easiest to describe in terms of what it's not: it's not self-critical, it's not oriented toward producing something or

improving myself, it's not busy, it's not loud. It feels like being
alive. It's where love is. As I've heard people say around here, you can
only do one process at a time, so when I experience love for myself,
I experience love for everything around me. My inclination as a
conditioned person is to avoid that, because it means giving up all
I have invested in who I think I am. Without meditation we get swept
off into things, get busy, won't take time to look. But when I
meditate for thirty minutes and I don't get up and there's no
escape, all my conditioning, my thoughts, try to take me away from
myself, and then I get to see how that works. There's a lot about
it that's mysterious to me, but it works: you sit on the cushion for
hours and hours and years and years, and a transformation happens.

◇

There are several ways that I get guidance from Cheri. One is in our
guidance appointments, where there is no question that I have a
compassionate person before me, giving full attention to me and with
full willingness to help me any way she can. She models self-acceptance
for me. I think that's probably the biggest thing I get from her.

Another way she helps me is by being the kind of Big Meany
far away, when she's not here. I didn't understand this when I first
came to the Monastery. I was here for three months getting my work
assignment notes and doing my job just like everyone else, and the
person who was presenting me with the guidelines was the work
director or the guestmaster. At that point, Cheri was just that
benevolent person who showed up occasionally to help me out, then
she'd disappear. When I got a job with some responsibility, being the
cook, I began communicating with Cheri over the phone, leaving
voice mail messages. Then I got my nasty notes directly from Cheri—
and hers are much nastier than the others! It was unbelievable what
I went through. She has lots of strong opinions and I have lots of
strong opinions, and I was always trying to make my opinions win

out, which never worked, or trying to sneak around and find some way to do what I wanted to do, which never worked either.

One time in particular involved buying groceries, which was part of my job. I was not supposed to buy anything that wasn't on the regular grocery list, but I'd had the job long enough that I'd forgotten about that. At the store I bought a couple of things I thought would be nice to have, and I mentioned them in my next call to Cheri. When she called back and left me my message, she said, "It is not okay to do that." She said that several times: "It is not okay." From an egocentric point of view, I'm constantly trying to prove to other people and to myself that I'm okay, and to have someone say something I did was not okay destroyed my whole sense of safety. A little thing, but it touched exactly the place where I was the most vulnerable, and I went to pieces. For three or four weeks I was sort of paranoid, me versus them, hated being here, desperate to leave, thought Cheri was up to no good, thought everyone was up to no good, thought everyone hated me, on and on and on.

Eventually, I suffered enough with that so that I didn't need to suffer over it any more, and I was able to leave it behind. I learned a huge amount in the process, about how life works, about how I try to make life work. I've heard Cheri say that all she has to do is put up her hand and people will knock themselves senseless against it. Nobody else I've come across is willing to do that, to not support your conditioning, to not try to make you comfortable. She was willing to point out to me where I was stuck, and that was such a huge gift—as much as I hated it at the time. There have been countless smaller examples of that since then. Because I've just gotten back, they haven't started up again yet, but they will soon.

This is the first sane place I've ever been. That's what it feels like to me. It's the first place I've ever been where everything, everybody is on my side, meaning the side of my true nature. Everything here supports my learning how to feel love and acceptance and to grow and to become who I really am—and who I am is something I never understood before.

From here, society seems insane. I hate to use the word conspiracy, but it almost seems as if everyone conspires to help everyone else keep themselves from having to be happy, from waking up and experiencing who they are. It's amazing to me that someone—the Buddha—actually figured out that it doesn't have to be that way. And the people who have figured it out for themselves since then, and that a place like this exists—it's miraculous.

I've committed to a year this time, and I would say that I'll be here for the long haul. What's nice is that I don't think much about it. I'm certain that life will provide me with the next step to take. Until then, I can just relax. Life provided this for me when it was time for me to come here.

Monks in the World

For many people, the fruition of spiritual training is to return to the ordinary world and offer one's being in the service of all life. The Oxherding Pictures, an ancient Chinese series of images representing stages of Zen practice, begins with searching and ends with returning to the secular realm, mingling with people, and, in those mundane interactions, offering—or, more accurately, being—kindness and enlightenment.

The return to the world traditionally comes after the culmination of a long period of monastic training. At the Monastery, those whose primary identity is as laypeople may make many "returns," living as monks during "practice periods" then living again in the realm of family, friends, and job. As indicated in the interviews that follow, Cheri is supportive and creative in finding ways for people who cannot become full-time monks to have the benefit of monastic practice. In a recent newsletter, she wrote:

> The term "householder" is an important one, because it acknowledges that there is a real difference between the practice challenges of a person living monastically and one living in the world of family, job, and society. Over the years people have asked me if it is better to live as a monk. My response has always been that practice is more a matter of sincerity than of lifestyle. In the Monastery, there is a

constant influence toward attentiveness. The environment is designed to encourage, if not demand, a focus of attention in the present moment. One wakes at a prescribed time, meditates, eats, works, meditates, eats, works, meditates until time to go to bed. No questions, no decisions, no debates. (Of course, there *can* be questions, decisions, and debates, but they don't get a person anywhere except frustrated, because the schedule is followed, period.)

In the world, nothing supports mindfulness—in fact, quite the opposite. Every day, every moment, one might be lured or distracted by any number of choices and options. Shall I do this, eat that, exercise or not, meditate, make a phone call, meet some need of a family member, do a few chores?

The real difference, to me, is this: the monk has the schedule and the monastic lifestyle to encourage her back to the moment. The householder has to depend on himself to bring him back to the moment.

These ideas are echoed in a talk by Archbishop Anthony Bloom of the Russian Orthodox Church in which he tells about fifteen years of attempting to live a monastic life when the monasteries of his country had been closed and he and other believers were dispersed across Europe. Without the support of an actual monastery, with no community, what did it mean to be a monk? How could three men living in various accommodations within cities replicate the stability provided by an enclosed monastery? They discovered, he said, that that stability must be found within their own hearts, in the knowledge that God is everywhere and that the Kingdom of God begins within.

The story of Bloom's professing as a monk is a wonderful illustration of that. Because his grandmother and mother were old and ill, he did not feel free to leave home. His spiritual director, however, told him that he could make his profession only when he came and said, "Here I am," without asking any questions about the future. After years of struggling with the conflict between his desire to be a monk and his sense of family obligations, finally Bloom made his choice. His spiritual director, however, told him that he could make his profession only when he came and said, "Here I am," without asking any questions about the future. After years of struggling with the conflict between his desire to be a monk and his sense of family obligations, finally Bloom made his choice. His spiritual director asked if he was ready to abandon himself completely, without condition. Yes, Bloom replied. He expected that their conversation would end with his being shown to his monastic quarters, but nothing was mentioned about living arrangements. Hesitantly, lest he seem concerned about the future, he asked where he should sleep. "At home," his spiritual director replied. "Continue with your life. Consider your mother as your abbot and everyone who needs you and asks anything whatever of your as your superior, and obey them unconditionally."

Once he had completely renounced his former life, he was free to return to it as a monk. It is easier, Bloom said, to be in a monastery. As a monk in the world, you serve not only your fellow monks and your teacher, whose interests are at least somewhat aligned with your own, but you serve anyone and everyone. And in doing so, you put yourself completely at the mercy of God.

◇

Tricia

Tricia's discovery of this practice was serendipitous: she and her husband moved two doors from the Zen Center in Mountain View. She liked being near a place where people meditated, she met Cheri, and for a while she volunteered to do yard work at the Zen Center. Soon Cheri (who had been doing everything else herself) asked Tricia if the Zen Center could hire her part time to answer the phone and pay bills. Eventually, Tricia worked almost full time in the office. Although not a monk, she considered her job, in which she worked closely with Cheri, as intensive spiritual practice. In this excerpt from an interview, Tricia described how going to the Monastery benefits her life in the daily world of work and marriage.

I go to the Monastery four or five times a year. As soon as I turn off my car engine, the silence hits me. It seems as if the very air is sort of pulling for us: *yes, yes, this is the work to do.* Everything there is for our training. Everybody is focused inward, doing the same work within themselves. The *sangha* experience is very strong. It doesn't matter if you do a job well, or if you mess it up completely; what matters is that you're paying attention, you're aware, you're compassionate. That's the way I want to live my life out in the world.

I'm married, and so as much as I love being at the Monastery, my place is in the world. I can come here and get very grounded and carry that into my life, rather than thinking that this is the way to live and trying to impose it on another person. For a while, I had set up spiritual practice as superior to any other way of life, something that made me feel special. I even set up meditation in opposition to my marriage: in the morning, I had the idea that it was better to get up and meditate than to make love. Now I'm more interested in how I can work out a way of living with somebody who doesn't necessarily believe that meditation should take priority over sex.

Before coming to the Monastery this time, I had been wondering, what would make my spiritual journey more enjoyable, less of a struggle? What came to me was, physical pleasure. Not a response you might expect, but Cheri is fully supportive of this idea. I wondered, aside from sexuality, what does that mean? As I've begun to explore the possibility of physical pleasure as part of my spiritual practice, I've had wonderful deep experiences of being in and with my body. Just how strong my body is getting with the physical work we do here—I feel it when I walk up the hills, and there's such pleasure in the awareness of that.

The first time when I was at the Monastery for a long practice period, I made a phone call to my husband every week, and after we'd talked, I'd walk back to my hermitage feeling so lonely and separate. This time I call him every two weeks, and I go back to the hermitage and light my fire and do my nightly rituals with great care and enjoyment, and then I do yoga and feel great. This time, I'm just being with myself and enjoying my own company. To just be with yourself—how many people have an opportunity to do that?

The Monastery is an incredibly special, sacred place on the one hand, and on the other, when you're there, you just eat and sleep and work and meditate. The whole issue of specialness, wanting to be special in someone else's eyes, has caused me an inordinate amount of suffering. I'm beginning to see how letting go that need for specialness leaves room for other things, now that I am opening myself to having so much more—both monastery and marriage, both spiritual and physical, all of myself.

◇

Susan

Susan dates her interest in the Monastery from a Zen-Catholic retreat she attended in 1992. Around the same time that she met Cheri, she met Andrew, her future husband. Before they married, she told Andrew that in 1995 she was going to quit her job as a campus minister and spend a year either as a Maryknoll missioner or at the Monastery. After they had been married a year, Cheri helped them work out a way for Susan to enter monastic training: for the first four months, she was at the Monastery, with home visits once a month for three days, and for the rest of the year, she alternated two-week periods at the Monastery and at home. Andrew was recently transferred to a location in the vicinity of the Monastery, and they have bought a house just outside the gate.

One of the biggest insights from the year I was here is what I call "looking with the breath." Before that, I always "looked" from my eyes, my head. Then, something opened under my solar plexus, like an eye— I called it my new eye. It was like intuition; I'd had very little experience with intuition before. But I realized that it is always there, and I can always get there, to that perspective. When I breathe in, it's like the eye opening. But the tricky part is, what I see is that there's nothing wrong. Everything just *is:* I'm sitting on the cushion, and the wall is in front of me, and outside it's raining. Seeing in that way, everything becomes clear, but there's nothing to—do.

Since the last *sesshin,* I've been struggling with moving through a sort of force field, a field of intense energy, to return to just being present. I'm sitting in meditation, I come back to the moment, and I experience this intense sensation—it might be labeled pain—and the automatic stimulus-response thing to do is immediately want to leave that experience, to do something to avoid it. It's not the kind of pain you have from sitting a long time; I don't know what it is, but I wonder if it's karma. To stay in the present, it feels as if I have to be in this force field, in which the pull is so strong to leave again.

Maybe this happens because being in the moment is so unfamiliar and uncomfortable. When I do manage to stay, that's when "looking with the breath" happens. The Christian image for me is gold being purified. It feels as if I'm being stripped of everything I hold on to, I'm being purified to move toward pure compassionate awareness.

Particularly in walking meditation, I've experienced being in that still place of just awareness, being able to see with the eyes of compassion: all is well. I'm able to sort of rest in the walking; it feels as if I'm not doing it myself, I'm being walked. Then something in me realizes that's happening, and I'm terrified. At that point, the force field is there. I suspect that the sensations in that field are just life, so full and charged and dynamic, and ego is terrified of it. The challenge is to stay present and move through the field. In a *sesshin,* it can get easier. That's practice; the more we practice, the longer we can stay, and the less strong the field is.

In my work as director of campus ministry, people find out that I meditate and practice Zen, and I get brought in to lead workshops. Cheri is going to lead a workshop with other ministers who work with me, and we're going to call it "Who Ministers?" Many ministers have excellent training and hearts of gold, but they don't have any tools, they don't have any way to drop the conditioned thoughts and be present to what's happening in the moment. We minister out of a desire to be good, to be righteous, to be what we think is loving and kind. But those ideas come from ego rather than from the clarity of being in the moment, being with our heart, being present to God. To know how to minister, we often turn to a restrictive set of rules: "This is the Christian thing to do; that's not the Christian thing to do," as if being Christian is acting in a certain way, like being "nice." Rather than letting God run the show through us, we try to run it ourselves, based on our conditioned ideas of how we should be.

An example is what happened with a kind of wild student on our campus, who was using drugs and alcohol and sleeping around.

She quit all of that when she got involved in a fundamentalist group, and she made a decision to be perfect, to be a "good Christian." But she wasn't perfect; she would slip up and have sex with her boyfriend, then she'd hate herself for it. When she got pregnant and had an abortion, she hated herself worse than ever, because good Christians don't have abortions. It was a hideously painful situation in which she thought she had to do everything through her own will power, then failed, then was convinced that she was a terrible person. A more compassionate approach would be realizing that "a personal relationship with Jesus" means letting go, coming into the moment and allowing ourselves to be transformed. It's not "doing," it's opening and receiving the compassion of Jesus. It's grace.

I want to share the tools I have, and to challenge ministers about what ministry means. I am interested in teaching people to risk *not* being a "good Christian" in order to reach an experience of true compassion and letting God live through them.

Last year I took Buddhist precepts. Yikes—I'm a Buddhist now! I'd been thinking, "I've been involved here [at the Zen Center and Monastery] for so long, they're probably wondering why I haven't taken the precepts. Do I really want to take them, or is there pressure to take them?" My fear was, "If I accept the precepts, does that mean that I am leaving Jesus?" I remember lying on my back and crying, "Oh, Jesus, why couldn't Cheri have been a Christian?" I just wanted it all in the form my ego could accept. But taking the precepts is like a sacrament in the Catholic church in that it is an external sign of an inward thing that has already occurred. Finally, I realized that it didn't matter whether I took them or not, because this practice is already in my heart. So I took them. I've never been conscious to a sacrament before (maybe semi-conscious during my marriage ceremony). In the Church, sacramental ceremonies come at certain times, you're told what to do, and you do it. The hope is that, over the years, the seed planted will grow into a tree, and often it does.

Taking the precepts was something I thought about first, and in the end it wasn't even a decision I had to make. The decision—the tree that had grown from a seed—was already there.

At the end of the precepts retreat, somebody said to Cheri, "You've given us so much—how can we give something back?" Her reply was, "Do this practice, and offer it to someone else." I think that's what I'm called to do, for people of my religion. I led an Advent retreat with Tony, who's also Catholic, and we're going to lead a four-day mission together in Texas. We will teach awareness practice to Christians so that they might find God present in every moment. When I work with both traditions together, I notice that I feel more and more called to explore the Christian part.

I remember Cheri saying to me once when I was preparing to speak at a church service, "Susan, are you willing to look like an idiot for the love of Jesus?" Essentially, that's how I feel about taking the precepts and being at the Monastery and doing Zen practice. Am I willing to be a Buddhist because I love Jesus? People might never understand this, but I died when I made that decision. It's definitely not what I pictured as the "righteous, holy" path, the right way to be a Christian. It is not what I would have chosen, in that it is not what ego wants. But it's what God wants. It's what God is doing through me.

◇

Greg

After their marriage, Greg and Jennifer left the Monastery and moved to New England, where Greg trained as an intensive care nurse and Jennifer continued her work with early education. Recently they adopted two children. In response to the request that he check the transcript of his earlier interview for corrections, Greg sent this letter.

I want to give you a current perspective on the effect of my monastic experience on my life these days.

When I spoke to you six years ago, I was at the beginning of a period of disappointment. The best way to describe my spiritual path might be to say it has been a slow and sometimes traumatic process of uncovering layers of disappointment. The first few years at the Monastery were very hard on my ego. I'm guessing this is true for many people. When the process of pursuing self-awareness begins, most of us become painfully aware of some very ugly parts of ourselves. Cheri's teaching, as I understand it, points us in the direction of making friends with the ugly parts and learning from them, coming to understand the roots of those parts of ourselves that are suffering. In my case, beginning to understand and feel compassion for parts of myself that were terribly disappointed (and suffering over that disappointment) made it easier for me to allow compassion to be directed towards others. What I was beginning to realize when I spoke to you was that during my last few years in the Monastery, I had begun to form a new "spiritual person" identity that was interfering with going deeper.

I know that not everyone has this experience. For many people, monastic training is the work of a lifetime. Histories of the lives of the saints make this clear. Many of them just let go moment by moment, and a monastery is a good place to do that. But the histories of the lives of the saints are also filled with those who had to go through all sorts of trials, tribulations, penances, and whatever to get to the simple faith and trust of the saints. In the unlikely event that I am remembered as a saint, I will definitely fall into the second category.

I was very angry and disappointed about the way Cheri treated me after Jennifer and I were married. I wanted her to treat me as a special person, or, more accurately, a *special* special person. (I understand a little more of what it feels like to be in Cheri's position now that I am a parent. Our children's idea of fair is to have exactly as much as their sibling, plus one more toy.) And, of course, I *was* a special person to her—just like everyone else who ever approached her with the slightest aspiration to spiritual practice.

It has been almost six years since we left the Monastery. Since then, we have moved across the country, gotten me through nursing school, bought a house, and taken in two children. Before I was at the Monastery, I could not bring myself to do these things, because I was so busy looking for the perfect life that I was paralyzed. Should I do this or that? Should I buy this or that? Who should I love? Who should I live with? What job should I do? I had some good hard lessons in the Monastery about how much I cannot control life and some good lessons about how to look at what needs to be done and just doing it. This was difficult, even in the privileged environment of the Monastery. It was even more difficult just after the turmoil of leaving the Monastery because I felt like I was cut off from the support of my teacher. Looking back on those days, I suspect that I cut Cheri off more than Cheri cut me off. It is comical to think about now, but I remember thinking something like, "Well, screw you, Cheri—I'm just going to do this practice anyway!" Which just shows how my conditioned mind works. Gratitude has never been one of its strong points. Memory is not one of its strong points, either, because as far as I can tell, continuing to do the practice is all Cheri ever hoped for from anyone.

So, what are things like now? I have a very stressful job. I am a nursing supervisor at a nursing home. There are always problems and crises. The main thing I need to do is to not panic. Our experiences at the Monastery with fires, freak snowstorms, building inspectors, disintegrating kitchen tents, etc., provided a firm foundation for my current experience. Another important thing is to listen: old people, mentally ill people, family members of residents, dying people, nursing assistants, practically everyone I deal with suffers from a severe lack of having someone just listen to what they have to say. Meditation practice really helps in this area. I smile a lot at work because I am very happy to be there. Before the Monastery, I was never truly happy anywhere.

Life with adopted children is filled with "happy, blessed opportunities." In other words, much of the time, it is really hard. Our kids need constant attention, limit-setting, information—they are personifications of my most needy subpersonalities. This is a big challenge for me, because my conditioned response to neediness in children is to crush it or ignore it. So, living with these children is like going to graduate school in compassion. I often think about things Cheri said about raising children. One time she talked about caring for her grandson and how she often did the wrong things even though she knew all the right things. She joked that every time she did something wrong, she put a quarter in his therapy fund. With our kids, it is difficult to know how to respond, and their therapy jars runneth over. Thank goodness our practice of compassion often prevails. However, if you are ever on a pond in western Massachusetts, and you hear some grownup in a canoe yelling, "Sandra and Guy, will you just shut up!—" it is likely to be

Yours truly,
Greg

◇

Phyllis

Asked by her religious order to choose between living at the Zen Monastery and her vocation as a Catholic nun, Phyl replied that such a choice was not possible, because for her the two were not separate. Seventy Zen students sent letters to the Order about Phyl's contribution to the training offered at the Monastery, requesting that she be allowed to continue there. After that, many of us assumed that the matter was resolved and that Phyl's practice and teaching would go on as before. It was something of a shock, then, to read Phyl's letter in the Winter 1997 Zen Center/Monastery newsletter, announcing that she would not be living the Monastery and would continue spiritual practice among her Order—and that that decision had been made based on guidance from Cheri.

To me, it's not one or the other, either Zen practice or Catholic practice. But by the time I finally was given that choice as an ultimatum, it had occurred to Cheri that it might be good for me to go back and "work from the inside." And once that occurred to her, it wouldn't un-occur.

When Cheri approached me about it—well, I was very resistant. My Order offered me a job at the Villa, a retirement/nursing home for sick and elderly nuns. I telephoned Cheri to tell her, and she thought it sounded like a good idea. But I definitely did not want to leave the Monastery; I insisted that the only thing I wanted was to be here doing this practice. Cheri said, "Then there's no problem, because you aren't here doing the practice anyway—not in that attached state of mind." As soon as that attachment became obvious, it was clear that going back was exactly what I had to do. Clear to Cheri, anyway.

I had nowhere to turn; I was backed up against the wall. When I hung up the phone from that conversation, it was about 8:30 at night. I went down to my hermitage, resisting like everything: *no, no, no, no, no!* I lay on my bed, and I thought, "Am I going to suffer like this for the rest of my life? If I leave here, my life will be total misery. If I stay—but I can't stay. If Cheri wants me to go, I have to go."

I remember lying there and it being dark and the stars shining through my window, saying over and over how I couldn't stand it, but I had to. I was watching it all, and then there was a change, a little shift. Somehow I saw clearly my attachment to staying at the Monastery, and I realized that I simply had to let that go, I wouldn't be credible if I didn't. Glimpsing just that much was like a little crack of light, but it was enough. Suddenly the resistance was gone, and I said, "Yes."

Then I was crying and laughing; it felt as if grace just poured into me. In that short span of time, it had happened. It was clear that I could go back to the Order, and there would be no problem. I ran out of my hermitage and back up the hill to the phone and called Cheri's voice mail, still laughing and crying. All I said was, "I can do it! I still hope it won't come to that, but if it does, I can do it."

I went back and began to think about how I could work it out. Now and then I would hope that God would intervene and say, "Okay, now that you've shown your willingness, the game's over, you don't have to go through this after all"—like Abraham accepting God's will that he sacrifice his son, but at the last minute being saved from actually doing it.

In fact, what came to pass is that I returned to live and work with the Sisters. And it's wonderful. I work with the sick and aged and dying. One of my best buddies is an eighty-six-year-old Sister who has Alzheimer's disease; to her I'm "that boy." We get along fine because we're both more or less in the present moment.

I'm still leading the life of a monk. I live in the vestibule of what used to be our chapel. It's a little room on a third floor—it's like an indoor hermitage. I use the confessional for my closet. Behind the altar is the sacristy, where another Sister lives. Above that is a shower, and we share that and a kitchen downstairs. The kitchen was originally a flower-arranging room, so it already had a sink, and now it has a hot plate and a microwave and refrigerator. I can keep silence living there. I go to work, and three nights a week I drive to the Zen Center, then I go home, go to bed, get up again.

I come up here to the Monastery most weekends. There was a time when I started feeling some separation, that I had one foot in each place. Even though I was happy in my life at the Villa, I felt I was missing out on things here at the Monastery. Of course, that created a duality and the suffering that goes with it. But later, when I was meditating, something switched, and I realized that I have to give myself a hundred per cent to the Sisters when I'm with them, just as I want to give myself totally wherever I am in any given moment. And then the suffering disappeared.

My work now at the Villa feels like a miracle. I went without any plans, not knowing what to do except be present to whatever happened. I certainly had no idea of going in there and making things better. It's a wonderful place, the nurses and caregivers are really good, but there is a lot to do and not a lot of people to do it. For example, there was a van that wasn't being used, and there was an exercise program but not much enthusiasm for it. My job description is assistant pastoral care coordinator, but I didn't have very specific duties. I took the Sisters to their doctors' appointments and just hung out with them, talked with them and listened to them and walked some of them around. I practiced being fully present, not *for* them but *with* them, because that is my commitment to myself, to be with the present moment.

After having been at the Monastery for years, my capacity for work is a lot bigger than what I was doing at the Villa. So, little by little, I started doing other things for the staff, running errands, fixing things. I would be asked to do something, and the next thing you know, it would be done. I was used to being a monk: somebody asks me to do something, I do it.

We created a special exercise space, and I bought nerf balls and a basketball and toys, and after Mass, we go into this room and just *play.* In the summer, we go swimming once a week. It's fun, we laugh, people enjoy themselves. One Sister with dementia is becoming more active, she's talking a little, and now she'll even go outside some. I learned how to drive the van, and how to work the lift, so those who are in wheelchairs can be taken places and we pile in and go on trips. Everybody gets into the act. If one person has the energy—"Okay, I'll take them swimming," or "Yeah, I'll drive the van"—then everyone is enthusiastic about getting involved, so there's a real synergy in it.

In fact, the place seems transformed, although I can't see that I as an "I" did anything. I attribute it all to what I call present-moment energy. To me, it's just another miracle of this practice.

From the Front of the Room: The Teacher's Perspective

Zen teachers are notoriously inscrutable, unpredictable, unsettling. They say things that seem not to make sense and things we don't want to hear.

Cheri has said that all she does is point out a different perspective on life and encourage us to discover that perspective for ourselves. She compares it to sitting in front of the room with a meditation bell between her and us. It's as if, seeing only one side of the bell, we assume it to be two-dimensional, and so we ask questions that have no meaningful answers. From our perspective, the teacher's responses are intriguing but often baffling.

The teacher's point of view, encompassing the whole bell, refers to dimensions of the richer reality that we don't see. Sometimes we get glimpses around the edges and become aware that there is more to the bell than we had realized. But only when we move to the other side of the bell will our experience of it be full and clear. The teacher understands all that because she has been on our side of the bell. So, in spite of all the forces that work to keep us where we are, she continues to answer our questions and to invite us to join her at the front of the room.

Being on the other side of the bell—that is, the other side of
suffering, or conditioned mind—the teacher acts from intuitive awareness. What may appear as inconsistencies most likely reflect a keen
sense of what will be helpful to a particular person in a given moment.
I count as a milestone in my practice the realization that clinging to
a literal interpretation of Cheri's words can prevent me from reaching
a deeper understanding, and that if what she says doesn't seem to
make sense to me, it's my responsibility to open my mind to what
it *might* mean, to open my awareness to the intuitive "yes" that signals
a match between her words and my experience. In every case so far,
I eventually discovered that Cheri was addressing something deeper
in me than I had known before, thereby leading me to greater
knowledge of myself.

Tricia, who worked in the Zen Center office for a long time,
speaks for many of us in the following description of both being
drawn to what we see in Cheri and learning from her how to turn
to ourselves with our yearnings for wisdom and compassion.

When I was first working at the Zen Center, I would try
to figure out what Cheri thought was important, and then
I would think that was important. But I also noticed how
something could be really important to her, and then if it
didn't work, or for whatever reason, she would just let it go.
So I could never figure her out.

I wanted from her what we all yearn for, I suspect: to be
loved unconditionally. Then at some point, I had a strong
awareness that I simply had to do that for myself.

Later, I watched myself move back to feeling, "But I
don't want to do it myself; I want her to do it for me." And
I'm so grateful that she doesn't. She models it and she
mirrors it and she is it, but we've got to do it. I think that's
the biggest blessing she brings: requiring us to grow up,
requiring us to save ourselves, requiring us to love ourselves.
As much as I may feel that I want Cheri to do it all for me,

I really don't want her to; she can't, it's not her job, and I'm glad she doesn't have any confusion or pretense about that.

What I love most about working with Cheri is watching how she interacts with life. She's the person I know who comes closest to completely living a life of the spirit. When everybody else is somewhat out of whack, the teacher is there with that larger spiritual perspective. If I drift off into unconsciousness, she will bring it to my attention, very gently, usually, not in a way that makes me wrong. She simply presents her perception, and I can either take it as helpful information or take it personally and feel hurt and angry and resentful. I do both, but more and more, I'm interested in the perspective she offers and in finding that same clarity within myself.

In the following exchange (which took place at a retreat), Cheri presents the teacher's point of view.

Student: I have been assuming that you know something I don't know, and that you don't struggle, and somehow I'll be able to stay under your umbrella, and your clarity will just be passed on to me. It finally dawned on me that not only does that diminish who you are and what you go through, but it is also a way of diminishing what I think I have to go through—I was hoping somehow to get away without doing the work. Then it hit me that that is not possible; the work still has to be done, and I have to do it.

Cheri: As you can probably imagine, I am aware that that kind of thing happens. If one person has some degree of clarity, other people tend to make them into an authority, put them on a pedestal. I have grave concerns about being in such a position. It serves no one if people feel that my doing this practice means they can do the bare minimum and enjoy whatever level of awakening I have.

I expect the monks to not only do the practice at the same level that I attempt to do it, but to surpass me in their understanding. There's a tradition in Buddhism in which the teacher helps the student up onto the teacher's shoulders so the student can have an even broader view. The ideal is when the student makes the next step, which is up onto the teacher's head, so that the view can be greater still. I would hope and wish that for every one of you.

I was recently with someone from a place where there was a very strong spiritual teacher who was the focal point of everything in the practice. When the teacher fell upon hard times and was asked to leave, the entire place fell apart. Of course, if people are doing what they're doing because of a person, then when something happens to that person, whether they fall from grace or die or whatever, the whole thing has to fall apart. How could it be otherwise? If no one has taken on the practice and made it their own, then everybody will just put away their cushions and their beads and take up the next thing—rolfing or gourmet cooking or whatever.

But if the practice itself is our reference point, it doesn't matter whether there is a teacher or I'm by myself. I still follow the same practice. All the same guidelines are in place; it's all internalized. So, I like to think of my role here as more of a groundskeeper.

A man called last week who had read all our books, and he wanted to come meet me, to see if I was in fact the embodiment of the practice. Phyl told him I wasn't here, but that we have a monastery that is the embodiment of the practice, and he would be welcome to come see it. Of course, that wasn't quite as interesting. One thing that makes me well suited to this line of work is that I can't imagine anything more annoying and unfulfilling than to have that kind of role in people's lives. I'm open to the possibility that I've missed something profound, but I cannot see how that would be helpful. Now, to have the *practice* in that position—yes. Always to have the teachings at the center of my life, yes.

Greg gave me the greatest compliment I have ever received, and one I hope always to live up to. Having sat in on many discussions when people asked me questions like, "What is it like to be an enlightened person?", Greg said that he used to wonder those things too, then after he was around me long enough, he dropped that notion and considered that all I am is someone who tries very hard to do this practice all the time. That's very good, because with that understanding, as Greg watched me do spiritual practice, if he proved that in fact I was wrong about something, he wouldn't need to leave spiritual practice in great disillusionment. He'd just say, "Hm, I guess she's not finished with that one."

Student: At least for me, your sharing parts of your experience reassure me and are very much a reason that I feel committed to this practice.

Cheri: Just a regular old human being. Good. Because if I turn out to be the biggest flake in the world of spiritual teachers, it's very important that that not interfere with your practice.

Ultimately, what we're closing in on is that we can't do this practice because of somebody, and we don't need to think of doing it in spite of anybody. We're just doing it. We're all moving along down that path to the best of our ability, and we always come back to ourselves and our own willingness and our own sincerity and our own compassion, so that it really doesn't matter what anybody else is doing. And then we can all inspire one another, we can appreciate one another's effort.

It's important that each of us do the very best we can. Not that we be perfect by some artificial standard, but that we work very diligently. Whatever gratitude you feel for this practice, that debt can only be repaid with the same coin. So, at some point, you will offer to someone else whatever you have found helpful.

Student: One part of me wants to give myself to a teacher, and another part wants to stay separate so I can evaluate the teacher. So there's no real letting go. I am afraid to let go because I might disappear. And yet what I want is to disappear.

Cheri: I know exactly what you mean. At difficult times in my own monastic training, when I would think that the teacher who was guiding me might be a true maniac, the one thing I went back to was that I knew in my heart of hearts that there was nothing in it for him. No one would choose the life he was living for self-serving reasons. If you begin thinking that the teacher has some suspect motivation, I would hope that you would consider that.

For me, the greatest risk was following my ego around through life. Trusting my teacher seemed not nearly the risk that trusting myself had been. There was nothing he could have done to me that would have compared to what I willingly did to myself moment by moment by moment.

Something I find extremely helpful is the concept of projection. Most simply put, that means that you never experience anything other than yourself. When you really get that, you will realize that you are forever unable to evaluate anyone but you. You can't know what I'm doing; you can only know what you *think* I'm doing. So, it's a constant mirror for you of your thoughts. That's one of the most critical roles the teacher plays—just to be a mirror.

In the beginning, the teacher will take the position of your heart, your True Nature. When you encounter the resistance and defenses that come up as your identity begins to be threatened, the teacher is that constant that you can refer to. When things get very tough, you can't always find that place inside that lets you know that you can do it, that it's not all terror and despair and so on. At those moments, the teacher is good mother, good father, cheerleader, and wise person rolled into one, who's there on the sidelines saying,

"You're all right, it's okay." And when the teacher seems to represent everything in life that is scary to you, the only thing you can do is go back to your original experience of that person being loving and compassionate, and acknowledge that what you fear is probably being projected from within you.

After a while, you have gone through the same process enough times that you can do it on your own: some difficulty arises, and you go to that place inside where you know that everything is all right. Then it is time for you to take over the role the teacher has been playing, which is to leave your conditioning and come to your True Nature. Now you will make that shift for yourself. Then when I say, "What do you want to talk about?", there's nothing to talk about, there are no problems, everything is fine.

◇

Cheri

Cheri's own experience as a monk deeply informs the spiritual training she offers. Here she relates how her teacher in effect "broke the rules" of the monastery to give her the support she needed to continue in her practice. Equally moving is her account of how she began teaching and how she continues to teach. After many years of directing the Zen Center and Monastery, leading retreats all over the country, and working individually with countless students, she still speaks in terms of her practice, not of having arrived anywhere, but walking ahead on the path she so compellingly recommends to us.

My family was not religious. I don't have memories of their even being "spiritual." I can't say, "They didn't go to church, but they had their own experience of God." Nothing negative was said about religion; it simply wasn't part of our lives. And yet it was very much part of mine—I was very drawn to religion.

By the time I was twelve years old, I had found friends who went to church, and I got them to take me with them. It was a new experience for me; I don't recall ever going into a church before that, even for a wedding or a funeral. When I was thirteen and fourteen, I was going to different kinds of churches, mostly by myself, kind of wishing for a particular faith. When I was away at college, I got engaged to a fellow who was Catholic, and I began taking instructions to convert to Catholicism. But I just wasn't able to do it. I couldn't make the rules and the structure fit with anything that seemed to me religious. I think some things are difficult to come to so late in life; it took more preparation than I had for those things to be understandable. Whether or not that was an advantage in my spiritual practice, I do not know.

My mother's death in a car accident when I was eighteen left me with something I recognized much later as a blessing: I do not take for granted that people I am with will always be here. I saw my mother drive away one afternoon, and I never saw her again. Being aware that such sudden loss is possible tends to make each person, each interaction, each moment very precious to me. And that turns out to be a great aid to focusing on what is most important and, of course, to living as fully as possible in the present moment.

Several years later, I became very unhappy, had what many people would call an emotional breakdown, and attempted suicide. When I woke up in the hospital, with serious physical damage, the doctor who had operated on me came in. I can still see him standing there with a cigarette hanging out of his mouth and a long ash dangling off the end (which fascinated me—I imagined him operating on me with that ash about to drop). He said, in this stern, exasperated, fatherly way, "It's almost impossible that you lived through what you did to yourself. I suggest that you find out why you are alive." And he turned on his heel and walked out.

It's interesting to look back at a time of being so unaware that an idea like "Why are you alive?" is like a light penetrating through darkness—and the darkness itself was something I had not even recognized. I was stunned by what the doctor said, and as I recuperated, I considered his question. I remember lying there in my hospital bed, thinking, "I have lived my life trying to please others, and I have failed. I simply have not been able to be what others have wanted me to be. I think what I'm going to do now is try to be happy."

Of course, my view of life up until then had seemed quite rational to me: hopelessness made sense, given the condition of the world as I saw it. The information I got growing up was that I should go to school, get a good education, get a good job, get married, have children, buy a house, have nice things, and save money for my old age. I thought, "How can those be important things to do in life when we don't know who we are, or how we got here, or where we're going, or why we're rocketing around in space on this clod of dirt?"

I was actively looking for anything that made sense out of it all. Why would you want to work your whole life to make money when you're going to die? When I looked around (now, of course, knowing projection as I do, this is interesting to consider), I saw such cruelty. It seemed as if one of peoples' main interests was to go to war, to kill everybody who didn't agree with them. It seemed to me that people were just mean-natured. I can remember thinking that if we wanted people to be fed, they would be fed. If we wanted people to have medical care, they would have medical care. I always identified more with people who were outside society than people who seemed to be successful. It was a long time before I realized that my questions essentially were the same questions that the Buddha had. If the world is the way it is, how can anybody ever find happiness? How can happiness be possible in such a situation?

When I decided that I was going to be happy, I had to figure out a way to do that, so I started reading philosophy. I read everything I could find. I concluded that a lot of people had the same concerns I had, which was comforting (because in Red Bluff, California, for a long time I assumed I must be the only one who had these concerns). But they didn't have any answers. The concerns were well stated, and these people had thought about them in ways that I hadn't, but they didn't have anything for me.

So, I went to religion. I was never attracted to the Old Testament. God goes around deciding who are the good people and who are the bad people and killing all the bad people, then killing the good people because he's mad at them, too. It seemed to embody the same insensitivity and cruelty I saw all around me.

But I was attracted to the words of Jesus. I still am; I am a great fan of Jesus. Of course, I have my own versions of what he actually meant, but I am pretty sure that he and I could sit down and have a conversation and be in complete agreement about what he was trying to communicate. However, I just could not buy the whole story. This was two thousand years ago, and the world had already been here a really long time; why all of a sudden at that particular point would God decide, "Now I'll get this woman pregnant and send my son there"? It just did not make sense. I could see the advantages of "believing in Jesus": since he is the one person who is the son of God, of course if you are connected with him, then God likes you better than everybody else. But that's nothing like what I understood Jesus to be saying.

Next I tried Hinduism. I remember reading the aphorisms of Patanjali, not even knowing how to pronounce his name. I thought there was a lot of good stuff there, and there was also a lot that struck me as bizarre. With the Sufis, again, there was a feeling of, yes! to a great deal of it—yes, yes!—but the packaging put me off. I looked into Native American spiritual teaching; I think I tried everybody, all of it. And each time, parts clearly had resonance for me, but I couldn't believe in it, I couldn't pursue it, it wasn't anything I could put my life into.

Then, I picked up a little book that I still carry around with me called *What Is Zen?* by D. T. Suzuki. I can go back to that experience even now, I can touch into it as if it's happening right in this moment: picking up that little book, reading the first paragraph, and excitement pouring through me. I was enthralled.

I knew then that I did not know what he was saying. But I knew *he* knew. And there seemed to me to be no packaging. My clear sense was that this is true, this is so, and that he (whoever he was, because at that time, D. T. Suzuki meant nothing to me) knew the experience I was looking for well enough that he could write it down in a way that I could recognize it. Of course, I did not have all those words then, but that was the insight, that was the feeling of it.

This was around 1970, and not much was available then. There was a small gathering in Los Angeles around Maezumi-roshi and at Mount Shasta around Jiyu Kennett, but I didn't know that. You couldn't go into a bookstore and find a whole shelf on Zen, and I assumed that I would have to go to Japan if I wanted pursue this.

I taught myself to meditate from a book. The sitting position it showed was full lotus; put your left foot on your right thigh, and your right foot on your left thigh, and there you go. I don't remember half lotus or any other alternatives, but it may have been that I was so zealous that full lotus was the only one I saw. I worked and worked and worked to be comfortable sitting in full lotus.

And I counted my breaths, from one to ten, then starting over. I didn't get it that you were meant to count breaths only while you're sitting on the meditation cushion, so I counted my breaths all the time, whatever I was doing, every waking moment. I remember making a thirteen-hour drive and counting my breath the whole way. Of course, I would get distracted when there was an interaction with somebody, but then I'd go right back to counting. It was a quick trip into the present moment, and that brought a level of mindfulness into my life that was very powerful. Because I was spending extended periods of time in the present, I soon experienced the extraordinary effects of that kind of attention: instead of being in a dark room and the light coming up gradually, as it happens with intermittent short periods of meditation, the lights came on quite quickly.

I consider it a real advantage that I misunderstood the book in that particular way. I suspect that if somebody had been available to teach me, I would have gotten the idea that you count the breath while you're meditating, and then I'd have gone unconscious in the rest of my life, which is what seems to happen with most people. They try to be present while they're sitting on the cushion, and the rest of the time is time off. But I didn't have any time off.

Another advantage was that because I had only the D. T. Suzuki book, I wasn't confused. I had one person's view on how to do things, so, as far as I was concerned, that was Zen. Today, you can pick up twenty-four books by twenty-four teachers with twenty-four different kinds of information and get quite confused. But I was blessedly ignorant.

Last night I was reading something about three stages of spiritual development. The first was described as the aesthetic stage, which is sense-related and the level at which most people live their lives. What is pleasurable is good, and what is boring is bad. The second stage, if I remember right, has to do with duty: doing the right thing, being the right person, even though it's boring or unpleasant. The third is the religious stage, and it is possible to leap into it from either of the first two stages. I think that is what happened to me. I had lived mainly in the duty stage; there was always a desire to do the right thing, to be the best person I could be, and I had never related to "it's unpleasant, don't do it," or "it's too hard" or "it's boring." When I made the leap to the larger perspective of a life of faith, the whole world of the spirit opened up, and suddenly there was so much more to life than I had ever imagined. Instead of being focused on the right way to slice a tomato, I had moved to having a sense of the inter-connectedness of all life.

The immediate effect was that I became a kinder person. Duty-bound people can tend to be unpleasant and unkind. In the name of goodness and rightness, they often feel the need to inform other people about their failings and are even convinced that God would want people who are bad, people who do things wrong, to be gotten out of the way. The expanded awareness I was experiencing allowed me to see that even though I was clearly a product of that kind of conditioning, because of the suffering it causes, it simply has to be deeply wrong. In becoming aware of a greater kindness—even if I could not always integrate that kindness with my conditioning—at least I had a much clearer sense of when those two were in conflict, and I knew which one I wanted to choose.

◇

As time went on, I incorporated into my lifestyle everything I could find out about what was expected on this path. I became a vegetarian on my own, because I understood that was part of it. It was difficult, because I was in a social framework that offered no support whatsoever. There was not necessarily any negativity toward what I was doing, although people would say things like, "I just can't see why you wouldn't want to eat meat." I was ill-equipped to deal with that kind of statement but extremely vocal on the subject, and I got into arguments and probably turned off a lot of people to this path. But keep in mind that I was operating in something of a vacuum.

I sat regularly, and I sat a lot. I tend to get carried away with things I'm enthusiastic about, and this was my passion. Several years went by, and at a workshop I attended, there was a woman who was Japanese. Thinking she might know something about Zen, I struck up a conversation with her. It turned out that she was a Baptist from the Central Valley of California. However, the previous semester, she had taken a class in religion, and as a guest speaker they had had a Zen roshi. She told me that the roshi lived at a monastery about twenty-five miles away.

That was so amazing to me, and so wonderful—that there was actually somebody who might teach me without my having to go to Japan. I got the roshi's name and number from her, and I called and asked if I might come and talk with him. A nice young man said yes, and we made an appointment.

They were just beginning the monastery then, and our meeting took place in a tent. It looked like something from Arabian Nights: there was a carpet in it and these little black cushions, which I had never seen before. The whole experience was like entering another world. And I didn't want to leave. If they had given me permission and a toothbrush, I would have stayed right then.

From my D. T. Suzuki book, I knew that when you meet the roshi, you need to be ready with the question of your life. For the two weeks between making the appointment and actually going, I agonized about my question. What did I want to know? Why was I there? What did I want from that experience? I thought I might have only one shot; there was no guarantee that I would ever see the roshi again. Now I can't remember what the question was, but it was along the lines of, "What's it all about?"—my effort at getting those childhood questions answered.

That first day, I probably spent two hours with the roshi. He was everything you would ever want in a Zen master. He was clearly wise, and he exemplified what I had known was possible all of my life, I just had never had it mirrored before—the kindness, the gentleness, the presence, the clarity, the compassion. Just walking into his presence, there was a sense of wanting to burst into tears. Being with him was like nothing I had ever known, and it was so clearly and absolutely a spiritual experience. We talked about things that I had never been able to talk about with anyone. It was as if he were reading my mind. In his responses to everything I asked him, he went so far beyond anything I had ever dreamed of.

I began going to see him as often as he would let me. I made it clear right from the beginning, in a way that I probably would not have if I had been more sophisticated, that I wanted to sign up, I wanted to join. I knew from reading my one book what a spiritual teacher was, and I knew that if the roshi accepted me as a student, I would be putting myself totally into his hands.

The roshi didn't seem to have any saving-the-world motivations, nor did he even seem to have any interest in offering the practice to everyone. What he offered was only for people who seriously wanted that kind of rigorous spiritual training, and it was necessary to prove oneself first.

There were ten monks, I think, at that point. (The roshi accepted only ten students at a time, because with more than that, he couldn't give them the kind of attention he felt was required.) They had come up from Southern California and were embarked on a process that will sound familiar to anybody who has been in our group for a while. They had been given a piece of property with nothing on it, so they rented a place nearby where they lived while they developed the land.

When I first came, all they had there was the tent, a mobile home, and a root cellar with a zendo on the top of it, if you can picture that: down in the earth was the place where they stored canned vegetables and projects they were working on and other stuff, and up on top was this little Japanese-looking meditation hall. That was where we sat, and the mobile home was where he lived and where we cooked and went to the bathroom. The tent was separate from the rest, so the monks could be around doing what they were doing, and the roshi could see people without being disturbed.

Every day I got up and drove twenty-five miles to meditation at five a.m., then drove back. I saw the roshi initially every two weeks, then every week, and as time went on, after meditation I would simply stay and meet with him for an hour. I would ask him about all sorts of things, and he would tell me. During that time, I was learning a great deal—most of all, learning what it meant to be a student, proving to myself the sincerity of my willingness. I changed my life around completely so I would be available to do monastic training. I moved to the little town that was closest to the monastery, so I could be available all the time. I would go over in the morning and meditate, and I would spend the day working at the monastery, and then I would go home, just as if I were a monk except that I didn't actually live there.

When I first started sitting with the roshi, a phrase he used all the time was, "It's not what, it's how." I had no idea what the difference was between what and how. We would be talking along, I would have some deeply meaningful spiritual question that I had brought to him, and we would get to a certain point, and he'd say,

"It's not what, it's how." I could tell by the way he said it that it was really important, it was the culmination of our discussion. It was a great moment when I finally got a sense of what it meant, although I still didn't see how it pertained to what we were talking about. My next point of progress was when I could tell we were approaching the place in the discussion when he was going to say, "It's not what, it's how." I still didn't understand it entirely, but I knew I was closing in on it. Then there was the jolt when I really got what it was that he was saying, and I realized that no matter what subject I brought up, it would come to that same thing in the end.

Each time I would have that kind of realization, it would seem so logical, so obvious, looking back at it. I had been trying to think my way through each one of those things, and I would get nowhere. Then there would be a moment of letting go, a moment of clarity, and it all would make such sense. Once you see it, you see it from both directions, but until then, there is no way to figure it out. It takes an extraordinary person—not in a personal sense, but someone who is extraordinarily fortunate—to have the combination of willingness and motivation and sincerity and intelligence and opportunity all coming together to be able to practice without that kind of guidance my teacher gave me. I know for myself, I could have wandered around for eons (and must have) with no idea even where to begin.

Walking in and sitting down and talking with my teacher, I had an overwhelming sense of being home. And that experience is what sustained me when egocentricity was screaming that I should get out of there, it was craziness, probably a cult, that he was insane or senile or an awful combination of the two. Now, I have great sympathy for him, because I know from my own experience that what happened to him probably was that he simply talked to way too many people and he said the same things way too many times, and it all began to mush together in an unpleasant little stew. But those fears about him made me seriously nervous at many points in my training. When that happened, I would go back to what I perceived him to be when I first met him; I would say to myself, "Wait a minute: when you were happy and everything was going your way, you thought he was heaven on earth."

After a year and a half of my begging and whining and wheedling, my teacher finally allowed me to enter the monastery. I was so determined because I knew that he could help me end my suffering, and I was desperate to do that. There were no mysteries about what it was going to be like. When he finally accepted me as a monk, he said, "Here is our agreement. I will find everything that you cannot stand, and I will rub your nose in it." I can remember thinking, "If I ever get to the point where I'm not afraid of this person, I will never be afraid of anything else again for the rest of my life."

I arranged for five of my friends to come meet the roshi. It was quite lovely; we all had tea, and he answered their questions. Four of the five began monastic training while I was there.

A place was found close to the monastery and set up for several of us to live in as monks. Partitions divided the space into seven- by eight-foot rooms. Each room had shelves at one end and a felt pad that would be laid out at night with a sleeping bag on top of it. The zafu [meditation cushion] was the pillow. There was a low table you could sit at on a zafu, and it pulled over your lap, so that's where you would eat and do projects. We ate in our own quarters.

There was such a level of respect shown for one another, very much the feeling that we get at *sesshin:* we're all here together, we're all practicing, there's great comfort and security, you're not out in the woods by yourself, and yet you are left alone to do your practice. Complete silence, no eye contact. We never spoke to one another; I never had a conversation with another monk, never. I knew what their names were, because the roshi addressed them by name. But that's the only information I ever had about them. It was my idea

of heaven. And of course it's very much what we have replicated at our monastery.

Recently, I visited another Zen Center, and someone there told me that one of the most difficult things for her at this particular place was that there was so much focus on relationships. The idea was that it is good to be in a relationship while you're training, because that makes it like life, and the issues of life arise. My reaction is to think that utterly bizarre. All of those life issues—to be social, to be attracted, to act on attractions, to have desires and attempt to fulfill those desires, to enjoy all of the things the world of society has to offer—that is available to us everywhere. Where can we get away from that? Where is a place to focus on the things that are *not* available to us when we are engaged in relationship, indulging our desires, interacting? Where is a privileged environment in which we can drop personality, not have to question attractions or acting on them or dealing with someone else's stuff? If we do not have that privileged environment. in the monastery, I am afraid we are not going to have it anywhere in the world.

In my monastic training, I saw nothing that seemed like a bad idea. It is true that from my perspective, there were times when I thought my teacher was a little harder on me than he really needed to be. However, that had nothing to do with the silence, with the solitude—those things always seemed to me like a gift. Were there times of loneliness? Absolutely. But there are times of loneliness in relationship, and in relationship, it is much harder to sort out what is loneliness and what is something else. Every kind of experience arose in the monastic environment, it is just that it arose against a backdrop that was clearer and cleaner than anything I had ever known in my life. As we sit in meditation facing a blank wall, it is easier to really know that whatever I experience there—emotions and memories and imaginary situations—all that is coming from me. That's what monastic life is like.

Sometimes I think about our monks, and the thought passes through, "Gosh, this is such a harsh lifestyle. Day after day, week after week, month after month, they don't open their mouths. They have no contact with other human beings except in these very structured formal meetings." And then I get out into the world, and I think, "Those monks are the luckiest human beings assembled anywhere."

◇

I don't know if people around here feel this way about me and their training, but I went through a period of being terrified of my teacher. He had said that he would torture my ego to death, and he did. It was *awful.* Public humiliation, nowhere to hide; if you said anything, you were humiliated for what you said, and if you didn't say anything, you were humiliated for not speaking. I didn't feel that he didn't like me or anything like that. I didn't feel that he liked me, either. I understood that whatever he did was part of the training.

One thing he tortured me about was my little dog Toughie. He would say things like, "You say you want to do this training, but you have to keep your little lap dog."

When I got ready to go into the monastery, I had another dog I adored, and I was able to find a home for him very easily. But nobody wanted Toughie, and I could see why. I got Toughie because she had belonged to some neighbors who neglected her and abused her. When they went on vacation, I kept Toughie for them, and they said, "If you can find her a home, give her away, because we don't want her." Well, within twenty-four hours I was in love—and I did find her a good home, with me. But I wanted to move to the monastery, so having Toughie was a problem. I tried everything: I put ads in papers and with the local pet adoption place. Some people called and said they were interested and mentioned signing up for dog training classes. I said, "Are you kidding? There's no way you could get a leash and a choke chain on Toughie. Obedience training

is not a possibility for this dog." In every case, the people turned out
to be obviously not right.

The roshi had never seen Toughie until one day when he came
to where I was living, and Toughie charged out, all of fourteen inches
tall, barking and growling.

The roshi looked down and said, "Is this Toughie?"

I said it was.

Then he asked me, "What does she do when you meditate?"

"Usually she stretches out behind me and meditates, too," I said.

"Does she always bark like that when somebody comes around?"
he asked.

I said, "Well—yes."

And he said, "She may stay."

I thought he was kidding; I thought it was another torture campaign, and he was going to say she could come with me, then at the
last minute he would say, "What are you doing here with that dog?"

But he stuck by it, with certain conditions. "She is not yours,"
he said. "You will feed her and take care of her, but she's a free agent.
If she finds somebody she would rather be with than stay with you,
you need to let her go."

I agreed to that, so Toughie got to stay. She was my best friend
through all those years. She was the only being who was with me
before I went into the monastery and during the time I was there
and when I left.

$$\Diamond$$

Many, many times in my training, my teacher required me to
confront things that I had been hiding and denying and running
from all of my life. Of course, when it got very difficult and painful,
I hated what he was doing, and I wanted everything to be his fault.
But, at the same time that he was requiring me to face those things
about myself that I liked least, he also was removing my own self-

hate from the process, showing me a whole side of myself that I hadn't known existed.

I had come from a violent background, and I would describe myself then as a rage-filled person. A great deal of it was in reaction to cruelty; most of the rage arose when I perceived someone as being cruel to someone else. Because of the way I was raised, I myself had a well-developed ability to be cruel, in ways that were just socially unacceptable. I am extremely attuned to people's weak spots, I know everybody's Achilles' heel, and I had no hesitation about using that information. That was the way I protected myself.

Early in my training, there was a woman at the monastery who would say cruel things, even when we were supposed to be in silence, things of an attacking or accusatory nature. Historically, my response would have been to verbally devastate her, but even without speaking, it was in my ability to make that woman so miserable that she would have left. I would have worked it so that the threat she presented to me would be removed.

But for the first time, I didn't want to do that. In my relationship with that woman, I could see my entire life: I grew up with people like her, and the conditioned ways in which I defended myself against that kind of cruelty were right there for me to see. I also could see how her conditioning worked, how she didn't mean to be cruel. I would guess that she was actually a sensitive, compassionate person, and, like me, when she felt threatened, she would attack and attempt to destroy whatever she perceived as a threat.

In my newfound expanded awareness, I felt a deep desire to be different in how I responded to that situation. But I felt myself to be in a horrible position, because being different meant I would have to choose to be constantly attacked by this woman and not defend myself. I could conceive of not attacking first, in response to a perceived threat (which nobody else may see), and I could conceive of not attacking in retaliation. But not even defending—that was a level of life experience that I had never had, never contemplated, never seen as a possibility. And yet I knew that was what I wanted.

I went to my teacher and I told him I did not trust myself not to get pushed to a point where I would again make the choice to be cruel in self-defense. I said I didn't want to be that way any more. I didn't know if it would be possible for me not to, but I truly did not want to be that way.

And the woman was gone. My teacher moved her to another place, and I never interacted with her again.

That was such an extraordinary response, on many levels. If my teacher had been operating out of the way it is usually done in monastic practice, he would have left her there and told me to deal with it. But by removing that obstacle, it opened up everything for me. He saw that I did not need a failure then, and he was willing to support me and protect me so I could make changes, not changes that somebody else told me I needed to make but that I knew within myself I needed to make and that, left to my own resources, I was afraid I would not be able to make. For him to help me at that point did not make me feel inadequate, it made me feel trusted. I felt that he knew I could do it, and he was supporting my going in the direction I needed to go in to prove to myself that I could do it. It was incredible mastery on his part. It was truly inspired.

For the first time in my life, I had no people to deal with, which in itself was mind-boggling. And for the first time, a relationship opened up with another person in which I felt understood, that someone was truly on my side in wanting me to have my very best chance at success. I knew at a profound level that my teacher understood my conditioning, my sincerity, and all the components of that. At the same time, he understood that this woman wasn't in the wrong—she was just doing her training, too.

I had felt an instantaneous connection with my teacher, and this experience cemented that connection, yet our relationship was never personal. There was a task that the two of us were committed to completing; that's what it felt like. Once that task was completed, there was no need or reason for us ever to see each other again.

◇

The friends who had come in with me left, and after the incident with the woman, there was nobody in the place where I was staying but me and Toughie. My memory is that the roshi just cut me loose then. I would go to meditation in the morning, but after that, there was never any work for me to do. So Toughie and I would walk all day long. I'd pack us a lunch and water, and we would explore the fire roads up in the mountains. It was the happiest time of my life. For months, I didn't talk to another human being, except when I went to town once a week to get groceries. The rest of the time I was alone, it was just me and Toughie, and it was heaven.

After a while that all changed; the roshi had jobs for me to do again, and I became more integrated into the monastery life. I began leading workshops and sitting groups, and I traveled to San Jose and Reno and Los Angeles to lead workshops, and that went on for maybe a couple of years. During that time things heated up; I was constantly called on the carpet, berated, accused of doing things I hadn't done— all those standard spiritual training techniques.

It was always obvious to me that my teacher was offering service, in assisting people to do this thing that almost nobody is qualified to assist people to do. There was nothing in it for him. He didn't get paid to do it. There's no power in it. And he did it with incredible skill and compassion and mastery. It was like the old Zen story about the student who asked a master to teach him the discipline of sword-play, then spent years being subjected to surprise attacks by the master, until he finally learned to pay attention. I was constantly on the alert. "What is he doing now? Is he just saying this to see if I'll get angry, or does he really believe it?" Always, he was training me to look to myself: What's going on with me? Where am I not free?

When people ask me how I decided to teach, I reply that I never did. I went into the monastery because I wanted to practice Zen. I began teaching because my teacher's approach to practice required it. Teaching was something in which I had no interest and for which I had no natural ability. But that's what my teacher asked me to do. We were sent out two by two to lead workshops for people who were doing this practice.

At most spiritual practice centers, you'll be asked what you know how to do, and you will be assigned to do that. If you know carpentry, carpenters are always needed, and you'll be a carpenter; if you are a lawyer or in health care, those skills can be put to use. My teacher took the opposite approach. "You're a carpenter? Good, we need a cook." "You're a doctor? Fine, you can work on the roof." If we are attempting to confront our conditioning, and we are constantly put in situations where we are comfortable, it will be difficult to see what we are looking for. If we know how to do something, we can just go to sleep and do it the way we always have, and although the same conditioning arises, because it is so familiar in that context, we simply accept it as reality. It is much easier to see how our conditioning operates when we move outside our usual circumstances. That is why we leave our regular life and go on retreat, so we can see ourselves in a different mirror.

Teaching was certainly not familiar or comfortable for me. A two-day workshop would often be halfway through before I could open my mouth and be sure a voice would come out. When I started to speak, I would be shaking so badly that I would come up off my cushion. This was a lifelong response: when I got married, I was shaking. At your wedding, you're the big attraction, everybody's watching you, and there I was shaking. I realized that if I put all my weight on one foot, I could minimize it for a time, then that leg would start shaking, and I'd have to shift. So, I had a history of this as an indication that I was in a situation in which I was not at ease.

My teacher wasn't fooled by anything, and after about six months, he said, "Now the two of you are going to share the workshops equally"—meaning that I needed to be responsible for half of what went on. I thought it would get easier, that I would get better at it, but it didn't and I didn't. I just hated it. After about a year, my teacher brought the two of us in and said, "Now Cheri will do the workshops by herself."

There were two possible responses to anything my teacher asked: "Yes" or "Goodbye." That is, I understood that in monastic practice, you do as you're told, or you leave. But I also knew that leading a group was completely impossible for me. I wanted Zen practice more than I had ever wanted anything in my life, and yet I knew I could not do what he asked.

I sat there for as long as I possibly could, and then I said to him— very carefully, my life hanging in the balance—"Roshi, it's not that I'm unwilling. I just can't do this. I don't know how." I tried to explain to him that a person could not be less suited than I was for any kind of teaching. So, I figured I'd have to leave.

But when I looked up at him, expecting that he might kill me on the spot, what I saw in his face, in his eyes, was pure compassion. This still brings up emotion for me. He looked at me and said, *"You will do for the love of others what you would never be willing to do for yourself."*

Nothing changed because of that; it was still awful. But I made a vow to myself: whenever anyone asks me a question, I will look within myself to see what my own experience is. That way, no one would ever ask me something that had been asked me before and I would not have already raised that question with myself, to the best of my ability. It's not that I would have an answer, but at least I could draw on the experience of having seen whatever was there within myself.

And, armed with that, I sallied forth. And never stopped. There was always somebody there asking me a question, and I could see their suffering, and I knew it was possible to be of assistance.

So, that's how I came to teaching. I have never learned to like it. I have remained willing.

◇

The whole point of being at that monastery was to train to be a priest; that's what went on there. Some of the people who had come in at the same time I did were being ordained. I wasn't, first of all, because it required not seeing my daughter again, and my attachment to her was something I would not give up for my spiritual practice. I don't even know that the roshi would have held me to that requirement, but it was perfectly understandable to me—the unwillingness demonstrated in my decision was the issue. Later, he and I had an exchange in which he misunderstood or pretended to misunderstand what I said, and he accused me of being angry. By that time, I could trust myself to look inside and tell what was operating in me, what was motivating me, and I wasn't angry. But he said, "Because you refuse to let go of your anger, I will not ordain you."

I was never ordained, so I am not qualified to ordain anybody, but also I am not interested in ordaining anybody. I've come to see the whole thing as irrelevant. In a practice of nondiscrimination, to discriminate among people in terms of outfits and titles and roles seems unhelpful. It seems much more in keeping with society than with spiritual practice. But thanks to my bad personality, I managed to get out of the monastery untainted, so to speak, by ordination. If you consider that I'm a person who has more or less devoted herself to not having any credentials at all, there's a way in which being ordained would be a sacrifice for me.

I feel tremendous gratitude to my teacher. It's like a kid and a parent: the relationship changes so much as the kid gets older, and my gratitude has grown and deepened as the years have gone by. I don't think he needs people to be grateful to him, I don't think he needs to know what a profound effect he had on my life. I'm just grateful for the practice he's done in his life and how generously he gave and continues to give something that most people cannot even begin to understand the value of.

◇

When I left the monastery, I had to earn a living. Going into a traditional work situation was not anything I ever had been interested in doing—certainly not after monastic practice. I did possess carpentry skills. My father was blind, and I was his eyes from the time I could walk around. I grew up knowing how to measure and saw and what nails go with what boards and how you nail them. As soon as I could swing a hammer, I swung a hammer. My father walked me through learning all the things he could no longer see to do, and since he did it all by feel, it had to be exact. As a result, I'm very attuned to boards being joined together perfectly. I had used those building skills in the monastery, and when I came out, that seemed to be something I could do that was as harmless a way of life as I could manage at that time. I contacted some friends who were remodeling a house and went there to work with them. And my daughter came to live with me, which was wonderful.

Once a week I would drive to Berkeley for a Saturday sitting with a group who practiced there, and once a week I would drive to Menlo Park to sit with a group and have a discussion. As time went on, people I had done workshops with before knew that I was out of the monastery and asked me to continue working with them. Eventually, I was going to meditation or offering meditation five nights a week and leading workshops on the weekends and driving back and forth to where I lived and worked, and I was getting really tired.

Finally, one fellow said, "We need to get a place so you can just teach, because I'm afraid you're going to wear yourself out doing this." We had an evening group which Phyl and Jennifer and Greg and some of the old-timers were part of, and across the street from where we met was a house for sale, a horribly dilapidated place. And we decided to buy it. Some people thought I was nuts, but most of them trusted that I must have some sort of vision that they didn't have. Because of my experience with building, it wasn't as daunting to me as it was to other people; I could see the potential there.

The house was on the market for $79,000, which was outlandishly cheap. We offered $80,000, and it was ours. We scrounged together a $9,000 down payment, and the mortgage was $720 a month, and after we'd done the deal, people were kind of hysterical, worrying about not being able to make the mortgage payment. I said, "We don't need to waste any energy worrying about that, because if we can't make the mortgage payment, they'll take the house away from us, and that will be that." People also were opposed to my commitment not to charge for anything, because they didn't believe that people would donate. But I was adamant, and, for the record, I was right: people were generous. As I've said many times about things like that, we cannot operate out of fear; fear and spiritual practice just do not go together.

We worked liked crazy to fix up the place. Grass had grown up inside the walls and out the eaves. Inside the house were ten cats and two parrots, who had been living there uncared for. We had to cut away walls to get rid of the cat spray smell. To clean the kitchen, I started with a shovel and a garden hose. The utilities man came to hook up the stove, took one look at it, and said, "Throw that thing away." Phyl scrubbed that stove for three days, and we still have it. In the end, it became a wonderful little house.

About three years later, we decided we needed a place to do retreats. We looked all over northern California and narrowed it down to this area in the Sierra foothills. When I saw an ad in a local real estate paper for large parcels of land, I contacted the agent, and we went to see the property.

We parked where the gate is now and walked in. When we got to the place where the building is now, I was standing underneath that big pine tree, and I could *feel* monks all around there; I could almost see them, it was that tangible a sense of people engaged in spiritual training and living on this land. I said, "This is it."

We went back to town and gathered at a little diner and discussed what to do, because we didn't have the money to buy the property. Phyl said, "I think we should just proceed until we run into something we can't get past. If that happens, then we'll know that's the end of it, and we'll quit."

We decided to take that approach. Pretty soon, several things happened that made it seem as if this was not the right place. First, because a cult in another part of the county had created problems a few years before, some neighbors didn't want us around and launched a fear campaign. One brought a suit against the fellow who sold us the property, against the county, and against us. We were in the local papers and on television all over northern California; it was quite a flap. Also, there was a rumor that asbestos had been used on all the roads in there, so we were concerned about whether or not the property would be safe.

But they tested and found out there was no asbestos. And by then we'd gotten to know some of the neighbors, and one family in particular went to bat for us. The County said that if we could get the residents along the road leading to the property to give us a green light, they would agree to it, and that's what happened. We still had to go through the lawsuit, but we won that hands down. The man who was suing said that we were charging people to stay here so we were a hotel, and we were charging people to eat here so we were a restaurant, and we were charging people for classes so we were a school, and this area is not zoned for any of those things. But, of course, we didn't charge anybody for anything, so the suit collapsed.

And here we are. We never ran into anything we couldn't get past. Twelve years later, the woman who sold us this land is handling real estate deals for people from the *sangha* who are buying houses just outside the Monastery. Some of the local people come here and meditate and participate in retreats and workshops and have become a part of our practice. For a long time, in fact, not many Bay Area people came up here with any regularity, so it would just be the monks and the locals. Now it's a busy place, with many people coming from elsewhere and nine people in residence and another one on the way.

◇

Ten is the number of residential students I can work with. That is one of many ways in which I have learned that my teacher was right. The quality of the training and my relationship with the monks is what's important here. If we have more people than ten, we end up with students relating to students. Now, it may be helpful in a personal growth kind of way to have students stumbling along and interacting with one another, being stuck in their conditioning and operating from that, and having somebody else pick up the pieces, but then we are back where we were, caught up in the melodrama of society. Nobody is going to give up their life to come live in silence in a hut in the woods way off at the end of a road to find the melodrama of society.

The difference between personal growth and spiritual practice is that one is staying a child in society, and the other is growing up. In this practice, people silently take responsibility for themselves instead of attempting to get the world to be a different place so they'll feel better. In the silence we look within ourselves, and we see how our conditioning causes us to suffer. We practice dropping that conditioning, coming back to the breath, coming back to the present, and ending the suffering. Period. It doesn't matter where we are or who's around us or what's going on, that is what our practice is. I can be in the middle of a war zone, in some completely insane situation, and it is still up to me to see how I suffer with that, what conditioning I'm dragging along that's causing me to suffer, then to let go of that so I can be free.

In monastic training, you learn that no detail is too small to attend to, nothing is insignificant. Now we have monks working in an office situation. When you answer the phone, you are representing spiritual practice to the person on the other end. If you're having a bad day, and you're cranky and unconscious, it is not okay to answer the phone in a cranky and unconscious way, because that becomes somebody's first experience of this practice. The way we put a stamp on a letter, the way we address the letter, the way we put things in a file, the way we vacuum the floor, the way we sharpen our pencils, all are worthy of our absolute presence and attention.

In that way, I think this place reflects the compassionate, mindful attention of the people who built it. People who come here sense that; it's in these earth walls, it's in the tiled floors and roof, it's in the glass panes of the windows, it's in the wood window frames, it's in everything about the place. That doesn't mean that everybody who ever did anything around here was completely centered. It's the sincerity of the intention that counts; the intention carries us even when we have lapses into mindlessness. Everybody who lives here experiences that, everybody knows when somebody is having a hard time. But what we respond to is their intention to do the practice, their commitment, the fact that they're here doing this difficult work. To me, that's the definition of *sangha*—a group of people who don't lose sight of the importance of practice, who support this privileged environment so that every one of us has the very best opportunity that we can to end our suffering, to awaken.

Epilog: Walking Outside

Fifteen people file into the meditation hall. They bow as they enter. Then they walk to their cushions, bow again, and take their seats. One person sits in front and rings a bell to begin and end each meditation period. Everyone else, including the small Buddha statue next to the bell, faces the walls.

The ten monks have been joined by five other people for an eight-day *sesshin* during the rainiest February in many years. In the silence of the Monastery, the deluge takes on an Old Testament ferocity, as storm follows upon storm.

From six in the morning until nine at night, except for meal-times, everyone comes to the meditation hall for half-hour periods of sitting meditation alternating with walking meditation. This is the heart of the practice: paying attention to the breath, the body, the mind. During *sesshin,* the focus is entirely inward: there is no read-ing or writing, no communication, no departure from the schedule, no exceptions.

As always, before entering the meditation hall, or the dining hall or kitchen or dormitory, everyone removes outside shoes and puts on slippers from racks near the doors. This, too, is the practice. (Finding oneself in the middle of the dining hall wearing outside shoes is a sure sign that attention has lapsed.) With each day of the *sesshin,* the familiar dance at the doorways, out of shoes and into slippers then back again, becomes softer, easier, more graceful, as awareness—of space, movement, others, everything—becomes more finely tuned.

One morning, the sky clears, and brilliant sunlight bounces off a dense layer of white cloud in the distant valley below. Silently, everybody puts on boots and goes outside for walking meditation. Step by slow step. Sloshing through mud and puddles and paths turned into waterways. Mindfully, fearlessly, joyfully.

The pines that had been dying are flourishing again, and giant cones are thick on the ground. The toyon bushes sport clusters of red berries. Around the flowering manzanita is the sound of spring: an insect hum. Deer crossing a meadow call to mind the Buddha's first sermon in a deer park. The practice bears fruit.

The monks look trim and vibrant and happy. The ones who have been here longest look younger than when they came.

◇

By the end of this stay at the Monastery, I am seeing monastic life as both more ordinary and also quite extraordinary: the monks going about their jobs, preparing meals and eating and cleaning up, sitting in meditation, and coming one at a time to talk with me. In all of it, they retain their personal identities, and yet, in the steadiness of their commitment to the moment by moment practice of compassionate awareness, they transcend that level on which we are all separate and inhabit instead the realm in which we are simply "life living," as they like to say. I think that most people who visit the Monastery share a deep gratitude for what the monks are doing and sense that, in some way, they are doing it for all of us.

From the Monastery Guidebook

The following material is from a guidebook made available to Monastery guests. The aim of the book is to explain the purpose and functioning of the Monastery in a general way and to provide information guests will need during their stay.

DAILY SCHEDULE

Monday - Saturday*

6:00	wake up	2:00	sitting meditation
6:30	sitting meditation	2:30	working meditation
7:00	breakfast	4:30	clean up
8:00	working meditation	4:45	sitting meditation
11:45	clean up	5:15	walking meditation
12:00	sitting meditation	5:30	sitting meditation
12:30	lunch	6:10	snack [light supper]

*Thursdays: Group discussion in Meditation Hall at 7:15 pm

*Wednesdays: Holy Leisure until daily schedule resumes at 2:00 pm.

Sunday

8:00	breakfast	12:00	lunch
10:00	sitting meditation		Holy Leisure
10:30	group discussion	6:00	snack

GUIDELINES

Key guidelines in maintaining the privileged environment:

Maintain silence.

Avoid eye contact.

Respect the privacy of others by not looking at people.

Do not go in or near anyone else's hermitage or campsite.

Be very mindful of not disturbing the habitat and environment of plants and animals.

Communicate only with guestmaster or work director using notes whenever possible.

Whisper when speech is required.

"Leave not a trace" by cleaning up after yourself at all times.

Other guidelines apply to specific places and activities.

A LETTER FROM THE GUIDE

The Zen Monastery Practice Center is a privileged environment established and maintained solely for spiritual practice. Here we have the opportunity to face ourselves squarely. In this place we are not social. We are not required to be personalities. We sit, work, eat, maintain our surroundings and physical well-being in silence, our attention focused inward, practicing mindfulness and presence in the moment.

The practice we follow here is quite strict, in the traditional manner of Zen. Phone calls are not allowed, and outside communication is discouraged or completely prohibited, except that which has been arranged in advance with the Guide. There is no socializing while at the Monastery, and silence is strictly observed. There are no opportunities to leave the Monastery grounds.

Our egocentric conditioning, which maintains the illusion of oneself as separate from all that is, functions through duality. "Potatoes are served, but I like rice." "I'm asked to cut wood, but I want to cook." "They do it that way, but I know it should be done this way." Our conditioning tells us that if we could make everything the way it "should" be (the way ego wants it to be), then we would be happy. Not so. The whole system of duality—attempts to control, belief in other realities in which things are the way ego thinks they should be—is suffering. Suffering ends when we drop everything that maintains the delusion of a separate self who exists outside the present.

At the Monastery, a schedule is set, and all must follow it. Changes occur regularly, and all must adjust to them. We are often asked to do things we don't enjoy or don't feel qualified to do. Each situation provides us an opportunity to see our conditioning for the suffering that it is.

The many guidelines at the Monastery provide a structure that supports and maintains the privileged environment. The one rule is that each individual practicing at the Monastery will use all that is encountered to see how suffering is caused, in order to drop whatever that is and end suffering.

All who wish to practice and train in this way are welcome here. We are grateful for every effort.

In loving-kindness,
Cheri